# THE

# WEALTHY

# RENTER

Editor: Dominic Farrell
Copy editor: Jenny Govier
Interior and cover design: Laura Boyle
Cover image: © VOVA/123RF.com
Printer: Webcom

**Library and Archives Canada Cataloguing in Publication**

Avery, Alex, author
    The wealthy renter : how to choose housing that will make you rich
/ Alex Avery.

Includes index.
Issued in print and electronic formats.

ISBN 978-1-4597-3646-7 (paperback).--ISBN 978-1-4597-3647-4 (pdf).--ISBN 978-1-4597-3648-1 (epub)

1. Rental housing--Economic aspects. 2. Rental housing. 3. Real estate investment. 4. Finance, Personal. I. Title.

HD1390.5.A84 2016        643'.12        C2016-903447-X
                                                  C2016-903448-8

Conseil des Arts du Canada   Canada Council for the Arts   Canada   ONTARIO ARTS COUNCIL / CONSEIL DES ARTS DE L'ONTARIO / an Ontario government agency / un organisme du gouvernement de l'Ontario

1  2  3  4  5      20  19  18  17  16

We acknowledge the support of the **Canada Council for the Arts** and the **Ontario Arts Council** for our publishing program. We also acknowledge the financial support of the **Government of Canada** through the **Canada Book Fund** and **Livres Canada Books**, and the **Government of Ontario** through the **Ontario Book Publishing Tax Credit** and the **Ontario Media Development Corporation.**

Care has been taken to trace the ownership of copyright material used in this book. The author and the publisher welcome any information enabling them to rectify any references or credits in subsequent editions.
        — J. Kirk Howard, President

The publisher is not responsible for websites or their content unless they are owned by the publisher.

Printed and bound in Canada.

**VISIT US AT**
Dundurn.com | @dundurnpress | Facebook.com/dundurnpress | Pinterest.com/Dundurnpress

Dundurn
3 Church Street, Suite 500
Toronto, Ontario, Canada
M5E 1M2

# THE
# WEALTHY
# RENTER

How to Choose Housing
That Will Make You Rich

Alex Avery

**DUNDURN**
TORONTO

# CONTENTS

# CHAPTER 1

## The Stakes Are High —
## Where We Live Defines Our Lives

We all have to live somewhere. Because of that, every one of us will need to make housing decisions at various times in our lives. When we do, there are lots of things we think about and focus on, like the size and location of our home, its cost, and its features. But our housing decisions are about a lot more than size, location, and price.

It's pretty hard to separate where we live from the rest of our lives. From a financial perspective, a career perspective, and a quality-of-life perspective, housing touches everything we do. It influences how we spend our time, how we fare financially, and how much we enjoy life. In many ways, how we house ourselves is one of the most influential decisions we'll ever make.

Understanding all of the ways our housing choices affect our lives is crucial to making smart, informed housing decisions. Not just for our financial success, but for nearly every aspect of our lives. This is true not just of the type of housing we choose. It is also true — and perhaps in a more significant way — of the decision of whether to buy a home or to rent one. Understanding the benefits — and drawbacks — to both is the first step in understanding the appeal of renting. As you will learn in this book, renting has many benefits, probably more than you ever imagined.

> Understanding all of the ways our housing choices affect our lives is crucial to making smart, informed decisions.

◎  ◎  ◎

Every person who reads this book will have his or her own history with housing. It may have taken place in just one house — it may have taken place in two houses, or fifteen. It could have been a farmhouse, a townhouse in the city, a condominium by the lake, a bungalow in midtown, or a combination of several. You might have grown up in an owned home or a rented one. We all have different experiences, but each of us grew up somewhere, and all of us have lived in some form of housing our entire lives. This experience is the lens through which we see housing.

I myself grew up in the suburbs, on a dead-end street that backed onto a ravine where I spent countless hours exploring and playing with friends. My parents raised us in a house they owned. My sister and I went to the same primary school, the same middle school, and the same high school. We had lots of friends, many of whom are still our friends today. We stayed in this house from the time I was two years old until I left for university. It was a great house and a great neighbourhood. And until I went away to school, it was the only kind of house I'd ever known.

Since I left home for university, I've rented more than a dozen places, including rooms in houses, apartments in apartment buildings, apartments in condo buildings, basement apartments, and detached single-family houses. I've also owned homes, in two different cities, and I've been a landlord, seeing the other side of renting.

So I've lived in many types of housing and I've rented and owned. I've also talked to family and friends about their homes. Having spent the last fifteen years analyzing real estate investments for everyone from pension funds, to the wealthiest Canadian families, to roommates, friends, and family members, I've helped hundreds of people make decisions about their housing. What I've come to learn is that, for most people, although the housing decisions our parents have made and we have made form the settings for our lives, we seldom think about the

As the biggest expense of our lives, how well we manage the cost of our housing has a greater impact on our cost of living than any other factor.

many different ways housing affects our lives. In fact, our housing decisions have much more of an effect on our lives than most people think.

Where we live defines how we live our lives. Our housing choices determine how long it takes to get to work. How much time we spend with our friends and family. If you have kids, it determines where your kids will go to school, where they play, and who they play with. It can affect how well we do our jobs. It can determine how much money we have for other things, like travel and the nicer things in life, such as cars, clothes, jewellery, electronics, and collectibles. It's probably the biggest factor that determines when we can retire and how we retire.

Housing is the largest single expense in life for the vast majority of Canadians. For those who choose to own, buying a home is the biggest purchase of their lives. For renters, the rent cheque is usually the largest monthly expense and over a lifetime is almost certainly the largest expense. As the biggest expense of our lives, how well we manage the cost of our housing has a greater impact on our cost of living than any other factor.

With all this at stake, how can you afford to not know as much as you possibly can about housing?

Why is it that so many of us spend more time considering which car to buy or which wireless plan to choose than we do trying to understand the type of housing that makes the most sense for our lives?

And I'm not talking about the time spent going out to look at five, fifty, or a hundred places before we decide on the home we'll live in. That's house hunting. That's the fun part. Whether you're looking to rent or buy, house hunting is what you do once you've figured out what kind of housing makes sense.

I'm talking about sitting down and figuring out what's right for our lives — right for our age, right for our family situation, right for our careers, right for our financial situation, and right for our peace of mind.

Examples of the choices people make are everywhere. I've got all sorts of friends who have made very different housing choices, and the effect of those choices on their lives has been profound.

- Andy lives in a small rented apartment just down the street from where he works. He loves the affordability, convenience, and time savings of a small, well-located rental apartment. He likes to travel, often on a moment's notice, and the money he saves by renting a nice but small apartment gives him the financial flexibility to hop on a plane almost whenever he feels like it. He never has to worry about who will mow the lawn, shovel the snow, or otherwise take care of his place when he travels. He just locks the door and he's off.

Because Andy's job means he might be transferred to offices in other countries, renting allows him the flexibility to react quickly to opportunities to move where his work takes him, whether for his current company or for others. It also means he can take bigger risks at work because he hasn't committed himself to paying a mortgage for the next twenty-five years — the kind of risks that will either vault his career to new heights or get him fired, like speaking his mind when he sees a bad decision or choice being made that he knows will hurt the business. Renting gives Andy the flexibility to be bold, and it's allowed him to be an outspoken leader in his field.

- Kevin and Alison bought a large, beautiful home with a huge back-yard outside of town. They probably took on a large mortgage (I haven't pried); if so, it will take them decades to pay it off. Kevin now commutes a long way to get to work and back. His eight-hour work day is actually eleven hours, including an hour and a half of commuting each way, adding three hours to his "work" day. Alison works part-time, close to home, allowing her to spend more time with their kids. Fortunately, their extended families aren't too far away, so they see them regularly and benefit from some very low-cost babysitting (a bottle of wine here and there). They have a spacious, beautiful home on a large piece of land — a great place to raise their family and a great home they take pride in.

- Jennifer and Chris rent a nice but small two-bedroom townhouse in an expensive neighbourhood where they couldn't afford to buy a single-family house. Their townhouse is close to lots of friends and family, which is important to Jennifer and Chris. It's also close to work, which means that, with their busy work schedules, they don't spend any more time than necessary travelling to and from work. And that means they can spend more time taking their daughter to the local parks and to visit friends and family. Jennifer and Chris have traded the space they could have gotten in a larger house in a more affordable neighbourhood for the opportunity to be close to friends, family, and work. They've also decided not to commit a huge multiple of their net worth to a home they think might not meet their needs in a few years if their family expands again.

The choices each of my friends have made have created dramatically different effects on their lifestyles, their costs, and the way they spend their time.

The right home for each of us is different. We can all imagine our dream home — our society is obsessed with real estate. It might be a beautiful country home with a veranda stretching all the way around the house, overlooking a gurgling creek. Or it might be a luxurious penthouse condominium downtown with stunning views of the city. Odds are that your dream home is somewhere in the middle.

These dream homes we have are normal. I've got a dream home. I've also got a dream car, a dream job, and a dream life!

This isn't unusual or abnormal. We're conditioned to admire and want beautiful places to live. Home ownership is aggressively marketed to make people want to buy homes in the same way car companies run commercials featuring their cars racing through hairpin turns with their engines roaring. Vacation resorts are marketed with shots of attractive people smiling and joking around on the beach or around a candlelit dinner. Cigarettes used to be promoted with ads featuring glamourous actresses and actors having fun and looking sexy — until lawmakers put a stop to that harmful practice.

This marketing makes understanding housing a difficult thing in today's world. There really isn't anyone we can turn to for good advice. The people who we typically ask about housing are generally unqualified or too biased to give us good, impartial advice.

Whether it's our parents, our friends, or our co-workers, or whether it's real estate agents and mortgage brokers, the people we look to for advice on housing generally are not very good advisors. It's not their fault. Our family and friends think they're giving good advice. But they're not likely to know much more about housing than anyone else. As for real estate agents and mortgage brokers, they stand to make money when you buy a house, and since that's the case, and because the more you spend on housing the more money they'll make, there's obviously a real incentive for them to persuade you to buy a big, expensive home. That kind of advice is a recipe for a bad housing decision.

As if making a decision about a home wasn't hard enough already, our perspectives on housing get further skewed by our society's consumer culture and the media's focus on housing as a status symbol — in other words, the idea of "keeping up with the Joneses." Media picks up right where the industry marketing efforts stop, profiling condominiums in London, England, selling for over £100 million, the beach house in Miami that a rock star sold, and the semi-detached house down the block that just sold for twice what it sold for two years ago. Housing can inspire envy and excitement. And there's a lot of money at stake.

On top of all that, there's government. What does government have to do with it, you ask? Everything. Government is coach, referee, cheerleader, and fan in the game of housing. In virtually every developed country in the world, governments have stepped into the business of promoting home ownership. They do this by changing the rules of the housing market. In Canada, this is done by offering mortgage insurance through Canada Mortgage and Housing Corporation (CMHC), the principal residence capital gains exemption, allowing first-time buyers to use their RRSP savings tax-free for down payments through the Home Buyers' Plan, and providing tax rebates on transaction costs.

Why would governments do this?

The reasons are many, and most are honourable. But by changing the rules, governments make it more difficult to understand the housing market.

Nonetheless, pro–home ownership housing policy is so pervasive and prevalent that it has become a part of the fabric of our society. It's enmeshed in our belief system.

Isn't it time to take a look at whether the old, conventional views on housing still make sense?

For generations, Canadians have dreamt of owning their own homes. Call it the Canadian Dream. Canadians aren't alone in having a dream. There's also the Australian Dream, the American Dream, the European Dream, the Russian Dream, the Croatian Dream, the New Zealand Dream.... Around the world, the belief in the value of home ownership is deeply rooted.

All of these belief systems revolve around the idea that freedom to determine our own destiny is best demonstrated through owning our own homes.

In fact, the dream of home ownership has become more than just a dream of a safe, secure place to call home. It a business. A big business.

All of this pro–home ownership propaganda might make you rule out renting, even though it's often cheaper — much cheaper — and it might just be the right decision for your housing needs. But until you know more about housing, you probably won't know if you should rent or buy.

It all sounds pretty scary so far, right? You might be thinking this book is about how evil the world of housing is and why no one should ever buy a house.

It's not.

What this book is, actually, is a celebration of the virtues of renting. Not in a home ownership–bashing kind of way, but rather in a way that explores the appealing advantages renting can offer. It makes the seldom-heard case for renting and helps you figure out if renting makes sense for your life. I'll debunk some of the myths about renting and discuss strategies for making a renting lifestyle create the kind of financial security and personal wealth so often associated with home ownership.

The world has changed a lot in the past twenty-five years, and even more in the past fifty years. Isn't it time to take a look at whether the old, conventional views on housing still make sense?

With this book, I hope I can help you better understand housing and help you make better housing decisions that will improve the way you live your life. You might decide to rent or you might decide to buy. But after reading this book, you'll better understand how renting can shape your life and whether renting is right for you.

# CHAPTER 2
## The Cult of "Why Rent When You Can Buy?"

You may not know it, but there are cult members among us. Not just one or two, but many. It's not your typical cult. There are no meetings, no official cult leaders, no rituals or initiation. Not even a clubhouse. At the same time, we can see signs of the cult all around us, if we only know where to look for them.

Its members are committed. They are believers. When they get the chance, they will try to get you to join the cult and adopt their beliefs. In fact, you might already be in the cult and you don't even know it!

You've heard the pitch. You might have even made the pitch.

The first time many people hear the pitch is when they are moving away from home, when they're most impressionable and vulnerable. It goes something like this:

> *"So, I heard you're thinking about getting your own place?"*
>
> *"Yeah. I think it's time. I just want a place of my own, where I can come and go as I please without having to worry about waking up anyone else."*
>
> *"Well, that sounds like a great idea. Have you thought about where you want to look?"*
>
> *"A friend of mine is renting an apartment downtown. It's nice. I'll probably look for something down there."*
>
> *"You say your friend is renting? That's too bad."*
>
> *"What do you mean?"*

*"You know that renting is a waste of money, right? You'd just be throwing away your money."*

*"Really?"*

*"Where do you think all that rent you'd be paying would go? It would go to paying down your landlord's mortgage!"*

*"I guess you're right."*

*"Look, when you buy your own place, you'll be making about the same monthly payments. Some of that payment is interest. But some of that money will go to paying down the mortgage. If you're going to be paying all that money, you might as well be paying yourself. Down the road, you'll end up paying off the mortgage, and you'll be left with the house free and clear. If you don't buy, you could pay rent for years and years and years, and at the end of it all, you'd have nothing left."*

It's a pretty compelling pitch. That's why it works so well. While you'll hear the pitch from many, many people throughout your life, the first people who usually give you the pitch are the people you look to most for advice: your parents, grandparents, aunts and uncles, friends, classmates, and co-workers. Because they're people you trust, it's easy to believe them. After all, what they're telling you sounds good. Soon you might find yourself a member of the cult you didn't even know existed.

These days, it's nearly impossible to go a day without talking, reading, or hearing about housing. Every media outlet runs stories about recent house price movements, sensationalizes the unrelenting demand for housing by profiling houses that sold for huge amounts "over asking," and reports the opinions of economists, investors, and bureaucrats on the subject of whether Canada is experiencing a "housing bubble" or if everything is just fine. Canada's housing market has even been regularly making the news elsewhere around the world. Stories in foreign papers, magazines, and websites have appeared, mainly focused on how Canada's housing market managed to avoid the crushing collapse of house prices that took place in the United States between 2006 and 2011, and how by most metrics Canadian housing is now very expensive.

At home in Canada we live it every day, where the unrelenting push to buy housing continues despite what every commentator agrees are high house prices, whether they think it's a bubble or not. This unwavering commitment to the cause is characteristic of cult-like behaviour and is what makes this kind of groupthink so dangerous. The unconditional support for home ownership seems so absolute that no argument or evidence to the contrary could change the minds of cult members, regardless of how compelling it might be.

Not convinced you're among cult members? Housing is everywhere you look, from stories in the newspaper to items on the evening news, from conversations on the street and in the change room at your rec league to chats at dinner parties and around the office. You can't avoid it, and it's even spawned its own entertainment genre.

> The unconditional support for home ownership seems so absolute that no evidence to the contrary could change the minds of cult members, regardless of how compelling it might be.

Have you ever found yourself watching *Sell This House*? How about *Holmes on Homes*?

There are dozens and dozens of shows available in Canada and all around the world dedicated to buying, selling, renovation, repair, construction, and any other aspect of housing.

*Property Brothers*

*Marriage Under Construction*

These shows get good ratings. People are fascinated not only by the challenge they face in finding the right place to live, but also with watching others work through the difficulties of figuring out where and how to live.

*Fantasy Homes by the Sea*

*Million Dollar Listing*

Housing can be a very personal thing. It's something every person on the planet has to have, and it can say a lot about who we are.

*Flip This House*

*The Unsellables*

The fact that good advice is hard to come by makes it even more entertaining to watch others struggle through these challenges.

*Flipping Out*

*Curb Appeal*

The potent combination of the personal nature of housing and the casino-like atmosphere of ever-rising house prices is nearly impossible to resist!

*The Real Estate Pros*

*Property Ladder*

Need I go on?

*Buy Me*

*My First Place*

Okay, I will....

*Property Virgins*

*Love It or List It*

Have I made my point?

You've probably heard of several of these, but not all of them. And you've probably seen at least an episode or two of a couple of them. Nearly every one of them focuses on some aspect of owning homes: buying, selling, flipping, renovating, or repairing a home someone has bought.

The point is that the cult is alive and well. It wants you to buy a house. And apparently it loves watching TV.

Not only is the cult alive and well, but it is successful. The home ownership rate in Canada is currently at an all-time high. Nearly 70 percent of Canadians own their homes, a number that has been rising consistently since Statistics Canada began tracking it in 1971 and has surged sharply higher over the past twenty-five years, from 63 percent to over 69 percent.

You're probably not reading this book if you haven't felt some anxiety about housing. I'll bet you've also felt a lot of pressure to buy a place to live and have had a lot of people tell you renting is a waste of money. You might already own a home. Part of the cult's promotion of home ownership is convincing people that owning a home is better than the alternative — renting — and that makes for a lot of criticism of renting. In fact, the positive and attractive features of renting are rarely discussed or celebrated.

> All of the arguments against renting appeal to our inner consumer, who just wants to buy nice things.

On the other hand, all of the arguments for owning, and against renting, sound reasonable and appeal to our inner consumer, who just wants to buy nice things. Selling the public on the merits of owning a home plays directly on a number of innate and learned behaviours: a need for shelter, a sense of belonging, competitiveness and pride, and the desire for physical and financial security. But sometimes when a sales pitch sounds a little too good, when it just doesn't feel right, there may be a problem. Listen to your gut.

Deciding to buy a place is a huge decision, and you shouldn't buy a place just because everyone else agrees that you should. There is nothing wrong with owning a home. It's not a bad thing. But taking a hard look at ownership reveals that it's not all it's cracked up to be. It's also not the only choice, and while renting gets a bad rap, it has a lot to offer.

I'm here to tell you that renting is okay. It's more than okay — it can be amazing! You don't need to feel bad about living a rental lifestyle. In fact, you can feel proud about it, and I'm going to tell you why. Renting can be a great financial decision, provide enormous lifestyle advantages, and allow you to avoid the crushing financial leverage and anxiety that comes along with huge mortgages.

# CHAPTER 3

## Repeat After Me: Renting Is Okay!

Renting is a beautiful thing, and don't let anyone tell you otherwise. The unsung hero of the housing world, renting is beautiful in its simplicity. Pay a fixed amount of money for the right to occupy a space for a fixed amount of time. It's that simple.

Some of the amazing things about renting are quite easy to see.

### COMMITMENT-LITE

Renting can be a casual relationship and one that you can change up with relative ease as your needs change. The length of a lease is typically quite short — usually one year or less, but often as short as thirty days, depending on how long you've been renting and what province you live in. That means that if your housing needs change, you won't have to wait long to move to a new place that accommodates you.

> Renting can be a casual relationship — one that you can change up with relative ease.

Maybe you need more space or less space. You might find the rent is too much or that you can afford a nicer place and the higher rent that goes along with that. Maybe you've decided to move in with a girlfriend or boyfriend. Or maybe you've decided to stop living with a girlfriend or boyfriend, in which case the ability to move quickly is particularly important. Having a kid? Or another kid? New place!

As life changes, so do your needs, and you'll often find yourself looking for something bigger, nicer, smaller, or cheaper. Whatever the reason you might have for moving, sometimes you can't wait to make a move. Renting allows you to move quickly and without a lot of costs.

## RENTERS MOVE FOR FREE! (OR ALMOST FREE)

If you're renting and you decide you'd like to move, there are no fees or commissions payable to move into a rental, and there are no fees when you leave. If you were to try the same thing as a homeowner, the transaction costs of buying and selling could be 5 percent or more for each transaction. If you buy a home worth two and a half times your gross annual income (a guideline that seems quaint and outdated, given Canada's house prices — do the math!), you could easily spend three months of gross income selling one home and buying another. If you bought and sold the average house in Canada, at just over $500,000, that cost could be $50,000 or more.

As a renter, you might have to buy some beer for a few friends or even hire a mover, but it's hard to see how that could cost even one month's gross income. And that's a cost that you would have whether you rented or bought. Also, for a number of reasons we'll talk about later, people who own houses tend to buy bigger houses than they would live in if they rented, and when they do, they tend to accumulate more junk. More junk equals more junk to move, which equals more expensive moving costs … whether you pay in beer or cash.

## ONE FIXED RENT EQUALS ONE FIXED COST

Renters agree to pay a fixed rent for a fixed period of time. As a renter, you know exactly how much you're paying, and you know how much it will be next month and the month after that. Having a single number for the cost of your housing makes it simple and easy to track. Life is complicated and expensive enough – why choose complicated and expensive housing?

With renting, you know exactly how much rent you'll have to pay to continue to live in your home. Ask a homeowner how much it costs for them to live in their house and they probably can't even tell you. They'll know their mortgage payment. They might know their property taxes. The cost of their homeowners' insurance? How about all of the utility bills and repairs and maintenance? How about the transaction costs of buying and selling? How much was the lawnmower and the gas you put into it? How about the opportunity cost? More on that last one later.

> As a renter, you know exactly how much you're paying, and you know how much it will be next month and the month after that.

While it's true that your rent can change over time, most provinces have rent controls that limit the amount a landlord can increase your rent and how frequently they can make increases. Ontario publishes a guideline that states that rent increases can be no higher than 2.5 percent per year for most housing. In Quebec, the legal limit on rent increases is calculated each year based on the change in the cost of property taxes, utilities, and maintenance or improvements (all things that would also hit homeowners). In British Columbia, the provincial government publishes a maximum allowable rent increase that has ranged from 2.2 percent to as much as 4 percent over the past ten years and that is calculated as inflation, defined by the consumer price increase (CPI) for British Columbia, plus 2 percent.

Home to four of the six largest cities in Canada and 75 percent of Canada's total population, Ontario, Quebec, and British Columbia have rules limiting rent increases that make renting a very stable, reliable way to arrange for housing without risking unexpected cost increases. Manitoba and Prince Edward Island have rent controls too, extending rent controls to almost 80 percent of Canadians.

As is often the case, Alberta is an odd man out among large provinces, imposing no restrictions on the amount by which a landlord can increase rents but restricting rent increases to once per year (increased recently from every six months). While this might not sound ideal — unlimited rent increases as frequently as every year — it's important to remember that, as a renter, you can choose to leave and find a new place to live if you don't like the rent increase. Aside from the hassle of finding a new place and moving your junk, there is no cost to moving.

## NO BUDGET BUSTERS

Renters don't have to worry about unexpected budget-busting repairs. Homeowners often silently, or not so silently, face the substantial and unexpected repair bills associated with owning a home. It could be a cracked foundation, a furnace that died, a leaky roof, or a special assessment from the condo board (if you own a condo — or strata-titled property, as they are called in British Columbia). There's an unbelievable number of things that can go wrong with a home, and it's impossible to know when they'll pop up.

As a renter, when you have unexpected problems with your home, it's a hassle. But that's about it. Usually it means a little inconvenience related to having a contractor come in to fix the problem. You might be without a working shower or a stove or whatever might have broken for a day or two, or you might have to be home to let the contractor in. But the biggest parts of the problem — the cost and arranging for someone to fix it — are the landlord's problems. As a renter you can even moan and gripe about the inconvenience the problem is causing. If the landlord doesn't act quickly to fix the problem, most provinces have a provision in their rental regulations that allows a tenant to arrange and pay for repairs directly and then deduct the cost from their rent payable the next month.

## BETTER LABOUR MOBILITY

When you choose to be a renter, you're improving your odds of finding a better job, one that might pay more and offer better career prospects. Why? Because you can cast a wider net in your job hunt, considering more jobs in more places. When you're renting, it's easier for you to move for work, and the cost of moving is significantly less. Owning a home

> Renting allows you to cast the widest net you possibly can as you look to build your career.

raises the cost of moving (in the form of high transaction costs), significantly increases the amount of time it takes to move, and reduces the likelihood you'll consider jobs in other cities or countries … or even on the far side of the city you live in, if it's a large city with long commute times. Toronto, Vancouver, Montreal, Ottawa, and Calgary have regularly featured on the list of the twenty most congested cities in North America.

Labour mobility is particularly important early in a career, when you're trying to establish yourself and haven't necessarily narrowed down the focus of your work. Finding the right job opportunity early on can radically change your career path and provide exciting and interesting work. Renting allows you to cast the widest net you possibly can as you look to build your career.

## YOU DON'T OWN YOUR PLACE

Saying that it's a good thing that renters don't own their homes might seem a little obvious and also a little counterintuitive. After all, the cult of "Why Rent When You Can Buy?" has so thoroughly convinced most people that owning is not just a good thing, but the only way to live. But the truth is, owning is by no means the only way, let alone the best way.

In discussions of the virtues of owning, a lot of the responsibility and risk of owning a home gets lost. Some problems with homes end up costing owners money, and often it's a lot of money. Other problems end up consuming a lot of time. Still others are things we can't do much about, but they irritate us. Even when nothing is going wrong, there is a certain cost related to the responsibility of ownership. Owning a home means spending time managing the home. Making sure the mortgage payments are made on time and that the property taxes are paid. Trying to figure out why the toilet isn't working properly or what that smell is.

If you rent your home, whether it's an apartment, townhouse, or single-family home, not owning means that you don't own the responsibility and risk of owning the home. If it turns out there is a problem with your home, like asbestos insulation, a noisy neighbour, a new garbage dump that's opened nearby, or a tall building that's been built across the street that entirely blocks your view (and all the sunlight!), you don't own that problem. What if the biggest employer in town closes down? That might make house prices fall as a lot of people lose their jobs.

Not owning can be a great thing. Don't like the way the neighbourhood is changing? Move. Want to be closer to the waterfront? Move. Have you

> Not owning means you don't own the responsibility and risk.

decided to travel the world for a year? No problem. Move your belongings into a rented storage locker and hit the road!

A lot of people feel the stress of owing a lot of money in the form of a mortgage and worry about whether they'll be able to continue to make their mortgage payments. The alternative is ugly — defaulting on a mortgage can mean huge costs. You could lose your entire down payment to things like transaction costs on the sale and legal bills, or, even worse, you could end up in bankruptcy.

When you rent, you leave all of those worries to the landlord.

◉　◉　◉

All right, Alex. That all sounds great, you say. But isn't renting still just paying someone else's mortgage? You're still throwing away all that money on rent, and at the end of the day you have nothing left to show for it.

Actually, everyone is paying rent, all the time. There are no exceptions. We're all "throwing away our money on rent." And that might actually be the best reason of all to choose renting.

# CHAPTER 4

## Rent — Something Everyone Pays. Always.

The backbone of the argument most people use to "prove" owning is better than renting is that to pay rent is to throw your money away. That a renter is simply paying the mortgage of the owner of the property.

While this argument seems logical and is intuitively appealing, it's an over-simplification that ignores two important factors: 1) the owner of the property has invested money into owning the property and is taking on the risk of the property going up or down in value; and 2) everyone who lives in a house (or mobile home or recreational vehicle or tent) is paying rent. Always.

That second point might seem like a ridiculous statement, so let me clarify what I mean. The word *rent* is defined as money paid for the use of something. For housing, rent is what is paid for accommodation — which can be an apartment, a house, or any other form of accommodation. However, any payment should be considered a rent payment if there is 1) a use or service provided in exchange for the payment; and 2) there is no remaining value after the rental period expires.

The most common rent that everyone is familiar with is the rent that a renter pays to a landlord. The renter signs a lease and agrees to pay a set amount of rent each month, and when the lease is over, the renter leaves with nothing remaining. This type of arrangement clearly qualifies as rent.

But there are three other forms of housing rent: one we're all famil-iar with, although we don't usually refer to it as rent, second, the routine expenses that apply only to homeowners, that might not be considered rent, and third, another you might be less familiar with.

The first of these other forms of rent is the "rent" that a homebuyer pays to a bank when they borrow money to buy a home. The money borrowed is, of course, a mortgage, and the money paid in exchange for the use of that money, interest, is in fact rent. The homebuyer is paying rent for the use of the bank's money over a period of time. The homebuyer then uses the money borrowed through a mortgage to buy a house — which means the rent they are paying to borrow the money is actually rent they are paying to occupy the home.

Every mortgage has an interest rate, which determines the amount of rent/interest the borrower pays to the bank each month, and there is also a principal payment. The principal payment is part of a mortgage payment that reduces the amount owing, and after many, many payments, eventually the principal payments reduce the mortgage balance to zero. The principal portion that reduces the balance is not "rent," but a reduction to the service the bank is providing to the borrower. Reducing the principal owing on a mortgage is kind of like shrinking a full cable package until eventually you cancel all together. Once the mortgage is paid off, the rent (interest payments) stops, and the borrower no longer enjoys the use of the bank's money.

The interest payment is a part of the rent a homeowner pays, but it's not all of the rent. To figure out what the other rents are, let's look at all the other payments renters and owners have to pay to live in a home.

Renters usually pay a specific amount of rent, but they also sometimes pay some of the utilities and other costs. The total of these payments should be considered the total rent.

For owners, the rent payments start with the interest portion of the mortgage payment. We can add to that the second type of rents we'll refer to as non-interest rents, including all the other regular costs of owning a home. These include property taxes, because property taxes are payable every month, and they are meant to be payments to the municipal government for things like schools, public hospitals, highways and roads, sewers, and other infrastructure services. Homeowners are required to continue to pay property taxes for the use of the services provided by the municipality as long as they continue to live in their homes and use those services. (Actually, you have to pay them whether you use the services or not.) Anywhere you live, there are property taxes to be paid as long as you live there. If you leave, you can stop paying them.

Another non-interest rent homeowners pay that most people don't think about as rent is maintenance. This one is a tough number to nail down because it isn't a set number and it isn't payable each month. In fact, many of the costs of maintaining a home occur only once in a decade or even once every forty or fifty years.

Most roofs will last between twenty years and as long as fifty or sixty years. On the shorter end of the scale, the caulking around a bath tub or shower should be re-done every five or ten years, depending on how much use it gets and what kind of caulking was used.

A new roof costs a lot more than a tube of caulk, but both cost money and they will need to be replaced. Anyone who has owned a home will tell you that maintenance costs happen a lot more frequently than you might expect, and there are a lot more mainten-ance items than you would think. Homes are complex — they are made up of plumbing systems, heating and air conditioning, at least one bathroom, a kitchen, a foundation, win-dows, doors, and a whole lot of things that

> It's easy to under-estimate the cost of maintaining a home, particularly because the costs are large and infrequent.

are painted. It is easy to underestimate the cost of maintaining a home, particu-larly because the costs are large and infrequent. A lot of them can be deferred for a long time without too much trouble. But if they're deferred too long, like waiting to replace the roof, they can result in much more extensive damage.

A reasonable rule of thumb for this cost is 2 to 5 percent of the value of the home each year. For homes owned through a condominium corporation, most of the costs of maintenance (but not all) are covered by the condo fee. Still, the condo corporation might underestimate the costs of maintenance and end up raising condo fees to make up for deferred maintenance. Or, if they wait too long, they might make a special assessment (a large one-time fee charged to all unit owners) to cover a major repair.

Insurance is another non-interest rent cost. Renters don't notice a land-lord paying insurance in case the house burns down, but they're quietly paying it. Homeowners rarely forget how much insurance costs!

So, in total, the rent a mortgaged homeowner pays includes: 1) interest on the mortgage; 2) maintenance; 3) property taxes; 4) utilities; and 5) insurance — and often a few other items (like mortgage insurance premiums, homeowners' association fees, security fees, etc).

TABLE 4.1

|  | Renter | Mortgaged Owner |
|---|---|---|
| Primary Form of Rent | Rent | Interest |
| Rent Paid: | to Landlord | to Bank |
| Other Rents Maintenance: | Landlord Pays | Owner Pays |
| Property Taxes: | Landlord Pays | Owner Pays |
| Utilities: | Landlord/Renter | Owner Pays |
| Insurance & Other: | Landlord Pays | Owner Pays |

Paying rent to a landlord is just a cleaner and simpler way of paying for the use of a home, compared to separately paying all of the costs outlined above. Homeowners are cutting out the middleman and paying all of the expenses relating to the home directly, including the interest payable when they borrow the money to purchase the house.

Now here's an amazing thing about renting: It's cheaper to rent a home as a renter than it is as an owner. Sometimes a lot cheaper. There are a number of reasons, and we'll discuss many of them throughout this book, but they include the fact that renters usually rent smaller places than owners buy; many rental homes in Canada are older than owned homes, and often that means fewer modern features; landlords are more practical and financially disciplined when they spend money on maintaining and renovating rental housing; and landlords often undercharge on rent because they

> It's cheaper to rent a home as a renter than it is as an owner. Sometimes a lot cheaper.

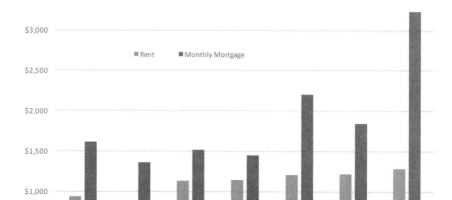

Monthly Rent Versus Monthly Mortgage*

*Average two bedroom monthly rent compared to average monthly mortgage payment, based on average home price, 5% downpayment, and a 2.4% mortgage rate with a 25 year amortization. Source: CMHC, 2013.

expect to make up the shortfall when the property goes up in value (which doesn't always happen).

It's true — in every major city in Canada, it is cheaper to rent a home than it is to buy a home.

⊙    ⊙    ⊙

What about when a homeowner pays off their mortgage? Are they still paying rent? Doesn't the cost of home ownership drop off substantially once there are no more mortgage payments? In fact, the costs of home ownership don't go down when a homeowner pays off their mortgage. Not even by a penny!

What does happen is that the mortgage payments, which were a part of rent, disappear, but they are replaced by an "implicit" rent. The implicit rent isn't a payment that has to be made; it's a payment you make to yourself.

Just like maintenance, it's a very difficult number to figure out, and it can change significantly over time. And because it's not a number you can see each month, it's dangerous. If you don't keep track of implicit rent, it can sneak up on you and become much larger than you'd ever imagine.

To understand implicit rent, think about it this way: When you buy a house, you take on a large mortgage, and over a long period of time you pay it off. When you do that, you've actually done two things. First, you've saved up a lot of money over a long period of time, and second, you've lived in a home.

If we separate these two things, you can look at the act of saving up a whole lot of money and look at other things you could do with all that money. You could buy bonds or dividend-paying stocks, or you could buy a rental property. All of which would pay you a regular income. All that money you would have tied up in owning that home could provide a lot of income,

> The amount of income you haven't earned because you've owned your home instead of investing in other things is implicit rent.

## TABLE 4.2

| | Renter | Mortgaged Owner | Unmortgaged Owner |
|---|---|---|---|
| Primary Form of Rent | Rent | Interest | Opportunity Cost |
| Primary Rent Paid: | to Landlord | to Bank | to Self (and Consumed) |
| Other Rents Maintenance: | Landlord Pays | Owner Pays | Owner Pays |
| Property Taxes: | Landlord Pays | Owner Pays | Owner Pays |
| Utilities: | Landlord/Renter | Owner Pays | Owner Pays |
| Insurance: | Landlord Pays | Owner Pays | Owner Pays |

and you are entitled to that income because it would be your money. That income — the amount of income you haven't earned — is the "opportunity cost" of owning your home instead of investing in other things. And that is implicit rent.

The amount of rent you pay to live in a home doesn't depend on whether there is a mortgage or not. It depends on how much the home costs. What changes as a homeowner pays down their mortgage is they gradually shift from paying the bank rent to paying themselves rent.

With the various ways homeowners pay rent, it's easy to lose track of the total amount of rent there is for a home. What makes it most difficult is the implicit rent.

Try this: Ask a home-owning friend how much their house is worth. You'll find that 100 percent (or pretty darn close) of your home-owning friends will have a pretty good guess.

Now ask them another question: How much implicit rent are they paying to live in their house? You'll get nothing but puzzled looks. Maybe 1 percent of friends will even take a guess at this number.

Now ask it another way: How much could they rent out their home for? You'll get more answers, but probably half will still have no idea, particularly if they live in a neighbourhood full of homeowners.

Ignorance is bliss.

Ask these questions of anyone who owns a home and lives in an expensive city, like Toronto or Vancouver, and then show them how to calculate the number. Once they do the math, they will be shocked by how much implicit rent they are paying.

Here are a couple different ways to calculate implicit rent. Depending on how you calculate it, you'll get slightly different answers. Implicit rent is an opportunity cost, and because it's an opportunity cost, the cost itself depends on what alternative investment opportunities are available. To figure out exactly what the cost is, a homeowner needs to actually change the way they are living — they need to sell their house, rent it out, remortgage it, or somehow otherwise invest the money they have tied up in their home in another investment.

First, how much implicit rent would a homeowner pay if they were to mortgage 100 percent of the value of their house?

To calculate this, take a guess at what the home is worth and multiply it by the mortgage rate you can get from your local bank. Any bank website will have posted mortgage rates. For instance, CIBC is currently offering a five-year, fixed-rate, closed mortgage at about 3 percent per year.

So, for an $850,000 house in Toronto (currently a below-average detached house price), the monthly interest is equal to the price times the mortgage rate, divided by twelve months in a year: $850,000 × 0.03 = $25,500 ÷ 12 = $2,125 per month. (Note that this calculation includes only the interest, or "rent," portion of mortgage payments.)

This will easily be the lowest estimate of the cost of implicit rent because mortgage lenders in Canada offer very low rates of interest, since Canada subsidizes mortgage rates through its sponsorship of CMHC. This estimate will also be low because lenders don't actually offer 100-percent mortgages — they almost always want you to put up some money for a down payment. If you borrow the entire amount needed to buy a home, the mortgage rate rises significantly ... if you can find someone to lend you all of the cost.

Another way to figure out implicit rent is to look at other things you could do with your money rather than own a home. For instance, in Canada many investors have felt comfortable investing retirement money in defensive dividend-paying stocks, including banks, insurance companies, telecom and cable companies, REITs (real estate investment trusts), and pipelines. Let's assume an investor invests in a portfolio of large, well-known dividend-paying stocks in Canada, generating an annual yield of 4.5 percent.

Under this scenario, a homeowner could estimate implicit rent by multiplying the house price by the yield on a basket of stocks and dividing by the twelve months of the year: $850,000 × 0.045 = $38,250 ÷ 12 = $3,187.50 per month.

If you aren't comfortable with investing in individual stocks, you could consider using the yield on the S&P/TSX Dividend Aristocrats Index, which is an index (portfolio) of TSX-listed companies that have shown a regular pattern of increasing dividends over the past five years and have market capitalizations (the value of all the shares of the company) of at least $300 million. In short, the index is designed to provide investors with a conservative portfolio of defensive, income-producing stocks. Over the past ten years, this index has provided an annual total return of about 7 percent (yield plus appreciation of value), and the current yield on this index is about 4 percent: $850,000 × 0.04 = $34,000 ÷ 12 = $2,833.33 per month.

Now remember, what we've calculated in the three previous examples — mortgage interest on 100 percent of the value of a home, the value of a home invested at a 4.5-percent yield, and the value of a home invested at a 4-percent yield — has just been the implicit rent or opportunity cost of a home. The total cost of "rent" for a home also includes maintenance, utilities, insurance, and other items.

Another way to look at the cost of an owned home without a mortgage would be to find a home for rent nearby and use the asking rent as an estimate. Depending on where the home is and how nice it is, the amount a home rents for could be a lot more than the implicit rents we calculated, in part because the rent a landlord charges is supposed to cover not only the interest but also maintenance, property taxes, and insurance, among other things.

So for our $850,000-house example, we found implicit rent was somewhere between $2,125.00 per month and $3,187.50 per month, to which we would add: 1) maintenance costs (2 to 5 percent of the value of the home annually, or $1,416.66 to $3,541.66 per month); 2) property taxes (usually 0.5 to 1.5 percent per year, or $354.16 to $1,062.50 per month); and 3) insurance and other costs.

At a minimum, in today's very low interest rate environment, an $850,000 home in Canada costs between about $4,000 and $8,000 per month to occupy. Regardless of the approach, those are big numbers. And those are the actual costs of occupying a home, whether you own the home or you don't.

## ATTENTION HOMEOWNERS!

Before we wrap up this discussion, let's do one more thing. If you happen to own a home with no mortgage, or just a small mortgage remaining, let's calculate how much you are paying in rent, see what else you can do with that rent, and see whether you are over-consuming housing.

- Take your house value and multiply it by 0.95, to reflect the transaction costs of selling your house. This is how much you could walk away with if you sold your house.
- Take that number and multiply it by the Dividend Aristocrats yield (http://ca.spindices.com/indices/strategy/sp-tsx-canadian-dividend-aristocrats-index), and divide by twelve to get your implicit monthly rent. A good conservative and rough estimate, if you can't find the current yield, would be 4 percent.
- Add to that number all of the other "rents" you pay (monthly costs of property taxes at 0.5 to 1.5 percent per year, depending on what city you live in; estimate of maintenance cost at 2 to 5 percent per year; plus utilities, insurance, and any other regular expenses related to your house).

This is what you are spending to live in your house, on a monthly basis.

Now that you know that number, there are two things you can do with it. First, spend a bit of time comparing that number to the costs of other housing options you would consider. They could be nearby single-family houses, rental apartments, condominiums (for rent or sale), or even housing in another location.

If the amount of money you're spending to live in your home on a monthly basis is significantly more than what your other housing options are, spend a bit more time thinking about what you would do with the extra money you would save by selling your house and moving to less expensive housing. If you were to save $1,000 per month, you could spend that money on four $3,000 vacations a year. Or you could take classes on something you've always wanted to learn about. Don't be shy — think of the most fantastic thing you could spend money on, and you could probably figure out how to pay for it with the sale proceeds of your home!

It might sound reckless to suggest selling your house to spend money on other things you enjoy, but what we're actually looking at is how much money you are spending on "consuming" the housing you are living in. Whether you spend that money on continuing to live in your house or on cars, antiques, or sporting events, it's all consumption.

If you own a home, have run the above math, and really want to improve your financial position, you could look at selling your house, finding cheaper accommodation, and, instead of consuming the savings, re-invest the proceeds of the sale in other investments, like the Dividend Aristocrats Index. Then you could re-invest the dividends from your income-producing investments, creating even further personal wealth!

Now for the second thing you can do with your monthly housing cost number:

- Take your total gross monthly income (before taxes) and add to it the implicit rent you calculated earlier. That was the number you calculated by multiplying the value of your house by 0.95 (95 percent) and again by 0.04 (4 percent). This is your gross monthly income, including the rent you are paying yourself to live in your house.
- Now take your total monthly housing cost (including property taxes, utilities, insurance, and maintenance) and divide it by your total gross monthly income plus the implicit rent you are paying yourself.

This is how much of your total income you are spending on your housing. I like to think of this number as the amount of money a person spends on consuming housing. It is consumption because every component we've included in this calculation is a rent — meaning there is no residual value.

CMHC suggests you spend no more than 32 percent of your gross, pre-tax income on your housing costs. CMHC's gross income doesn't include implicit rent in either your gross income or your housing costs. I think that's because the measure is designed to determine whether a person can make the monthly payments required to stay current on their mortgage.

However, the test we just calculated does ask you to include the implied rent you are paying. In doing so, it is designed to show you how much you are spending of all the possible income you could be earning on housing. It is also designed to make you question, once you know that number, whether you want to be spending as much of your income on housing as you are.

Figuring out how much of your income you're spending on housing is so much simpler for renters, and I think that's one of the reasons renters usually don't get in over their heads with housing costs. For renters, take your rent, plus any utilities you pay, and divide it by your gross monthly income to determine how much of your total income you're paying on housing.

Now both renters and owners have their numbers.

If the number you calculated is over 50 percent, you should probably spend some time looking into whether the housing you are spending so much on is really as important to you as the percentage of your income it is consuming. You could very well find that there are lots of other things you might prefer to spend your money on.

If the number is between 32 and 50 percent, then you are above the upper limit of what CMHC recommends you should be spending on your housing. That might be fine with you, if you really like the home you have and don't want to move. But it might also mean there are some significant savings you could find by moving to less expensive housing.

If you are under 32 percent, congratulations! You have made housing decisions that have you spending less than the maximum recommended amount, according to CMHC. This puts you on the safe side of disastrous, in terms of consuming housing you can afford. As we'll discuss later on, if you want to build wealth, there are much better things to spend your money on than housing. Minimizing consumption of housing is crucial to building wealth.

This chapter has had quite a bit of math, and I know not everyone loves math. I don't even love math. But it's an important tool. The key idea of this chapter is that, just because homeowners aren't paying rent to a landlord, it doesn't mean they aren't paying rent. They just pay rent to themselves. And when you pay rent to yourself, it's easy to lose track of how much rent you are paying, and you might end up over-consuming housing.

If you're still having trouble with the idea of implicit rent or are dismissing it as "interesting in theory, but not a real cost," you should know that it's not just me who recognizes implicit rent as a real cost. If you live in Switzerland and you own your home, you have to pay taxes on the implied rent you are receiving, as the owner of the house, paid to you, from you, the tenant in the house. Fortunately for Swiss taxpayers, they also get to deduct all of the costs of the house, including mortgage interest, from that implicit rent income they receive from themselves.

# CHAPTER 5

## The Canadian Housing Market

Canada is a nation of homeowners, for the most part, with just 30 percent of households being renters. House prices have been rising rapidly in recent years, which means a lot of these homeowners have seen the value of their homes rise, lifting their net worth. However, we also know something else has been happening that a lot of these homeowners probably haven't noticed: Their rent has been going up. And up a lot!

Just because 70 percent of Canadians own their own home doesn't mean 70 percent of Canadians don't pay rent. What it does mean is that the vast majority of that 70 percent probably has no idea how much their rent has gone up in recent years, instead focusing on how much more their home is worth.

Everyone needs to live somewhere. Canadians still need to live in apartments, townhouses, semi-detached houses, and single-family homes. But Canadians don't *need* to own.

However, more Canadians own their homes today than at any point in history — and this is true despite the fact that prices have risen considerably over the last few decades, to such a degree that many experts think Canada's housing market is significantly overvalued. Why has home ownership been rising? Government programs encouraging home ownership are part of the answer. But I think a big reason for rising home ownership rates is that it has been a winning strategy. As I just noted, house prices have been rising sharply for a long time. And everyone who has owned has made out like a bandit! (Or so says the common wisdom.)

## Average Canadian Home Price

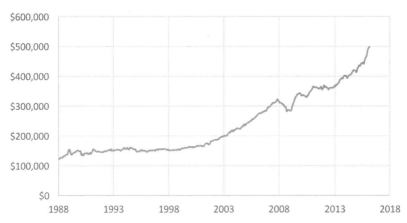

Source: Canadian Real Estate Association (CREA).

The good news is that Canadian homeowners have seen the value of their homes rise, creating significant wealth. The bad news is that house prices are high. If you haven't heard, not only are Canada's rising house prices seen as expensive by Canadians, but a good number of experts from around the world have voiced concern about our house prices.

- Robert Shiller, co-creator of the S&P/Case-Shiller U.S. National Home Price Index, Nobel laureate, and Yale economist, began calling for a correction in Canadian house prices in 2011.
- Goldman Sachs warned of an overheated Canadian housing market in 2013 and 2014.

Some of the others who have expressed concern about inflated prices in Canada's housing market include the following:

- The International Monetary Fund (IMF) — 2013, 2014
- Paul Krugman, Nobel prize–winning economist, City University of New York economist (2013)

- Pimco, the world's largest bond fund manager, with $1.4 trillion under management (2014)
- Deutsche Bank's chief economist, Torsten Slok (2015)
- Fitch Ratings, the global credit ratings and research company (2014)
- The Organization for Economic Co-operation and Development (OECD) — 2013
- Bank of Canada — 2011, 2012, 2013, 2014, and 2015
- Canada Mortgage Housing Corporation (CMHC)

So what has gotten all of these global authorities worried about Canada's house prices? Lots of concerning statistics and comparisons are being made to the U.S. housing market. Canadian house prices have risen at a pretty high rate over the past twenty years.

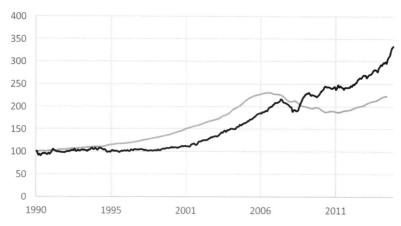

## Canadian Home Prices Outpace U.S. Home Prices

Source: CREA, U.S. Federal Housing Finance Agency.

House prices haven't just been going up in absolute dollar terms, they've also been rising relative to incomes.

## Canada: Price to Income Multiple

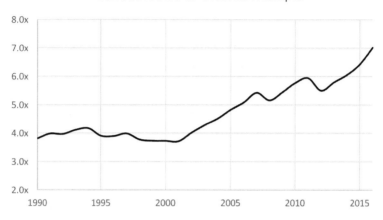

Source: CMHC, CREA.

House price increases have also outpaced growth in the cost of renting.

## Canada: Price to Rent Multiple

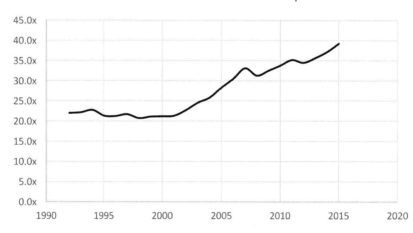

Source: CMHC, CREA.

At the same time, Canada's per capita debt levels have risen to record highs, eclipsing the levels seen among American's at the peak in 2007.

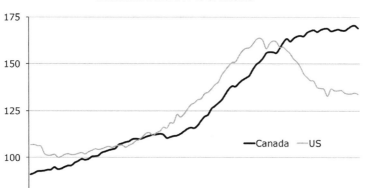

Household Debt As A % Of Income

Source: Statistics Canada, Federal Reserve Board.

Perhaps the most disturbing thing about the above chart is that the interest payments Canadians now make on all of that debt don't include the implicit rent the 70 percent of Canadians who own their own homes probably aren't even aware they are paying.

Look at what these five charts we've just seen say: 1) House prices are at record highs in terms of dollar values; 2) House prices in Canada continued to rise significantly after U.S. house prices dropped nearly 20 percent across the country; 3) Canadian home prices are at record highs relative to income, having grown dramatically faster than incomes over the past decade and a half; 4) Canadian home prices are at record highs relative to rents, having grown dramatically faster than rents over the past decade and a half; 5) Canadians are carrying dramatically more household debt as a percentage of income than at any time in modern history. If you take an objective look at those statistics, it's hard to come to any other conclusion than that housing in Canada is quite expensive. There are arguments on both sides of the debate of whether house prices will keep rising or whether they will fall. Whatever happens, whether house prices fall or whether they remain expensive, the prospects

> It's hard to come to any other conclusion than that housing in Canada is quite expensive.

aren't good if you're thinking about buying a home (unless, of course, you wait for a really large correction before buying).

While it might sound a little counterintuitive, further increases to house prices in expensive cities like Vancouver and Toronto aren't very good news for potential home buyers, as prices are already very expensive compared to historical levels. First-time homebuyers today are more saddled with debt than at any time in the past twenty-five years, leaving them committing to decades of payments with lesser prospects of higher prices in the future than earlier buyers.

Beyond all of the Canadians who might be considering buying a home, this situation isn't good for Canada. The 70 percent of Canadians who own their homes have huge portions of their wealth tied up in expensive assets that might deliver modestly positive returns over the next several years, or they might deliver negative returns. Neither would be as good as a cheap housing market in which the majority of Canadians could spend less on housing, and expect better odds of increases in house prices to boost their net worth and provide a higher return on their largest asset.

The run-up in house prices had been looking a little more reasonable when U.S. house prices were rising alongside Canadian house prices in the early 2000s. At least we had company … until the U.S. housing market collapsed in 2006. The magnitude of that crash, and similarities between pricing levels and indebtedness in Canada today and the United States just prior to their housing crash, have many people questioning whether the gains in Canadian house prices can persist.

Low interest rates have played a significant part in rising house prices, allowing each dollar of interest paid to cover more and more mortgage debt. Interest rates have fallen dramatically over the past twenty and thirty years. Using the same monthly mortgage payment, today's five-year fixed mortgage at 2.4 percent covers 72.5-percent more mortgage balance than the same payment covered as recently as the year 2000, when five-year mortgages were 8 percent. Not only that, but the total interest paid over the life of a twenty-five-year mortgage at today's rates would be half the amount paid on an 8-percent mortgage despite the mortgage amount being 72.5 percent larger. If you think mortgage payments are scary now, ask someone who owned a home in the early 1980s how crazy mortgage payments were when interest rates were massively higher, reaching over 20 percent.

If you assume Canadians are buying houses based on how much monthly payment they can afford, the decline in interest rates could account for 72.5-percent higher house prices since 2000, compared to the actual ~200-percent increase in the average Canadian house price since then.

This is a point that is often used to argue for a pending Canadian housing crash. The worry is that if interest rates were to rise back up to an 8-percent five-year mortgage, house prices would have to decline to offset the increase that lower interest rates helped move higher, to maintain roughly similar mortgage payments, which in theory could result in a 42-percent decline in average house prices.

It seems pretty far-fetched for interest rates to rise to 8 percent in the near future, but you never know. Nevertheless, interest rates don't need to go to 8 percent to hurt demand for home ownership.

As house prices have continued to rise, it's not surprising that ownership rates have been rising. The positive impacts of a rising ownership rate and falling interest rates on house prices are pretty self-explanatory. It's a positive feedback loop, with rising prices encouraging more people to "invest" in home ownership, resulting in more demand, which ultimately supports higher prices.

It's also pretty easy to understand that if ownership rates were to stop rising or begin to fall, and if interest rates were to stop falling and even rise, house prices might start to fall.

What might be less easy to see is the unique physical structure of Canada's housing markets and how that affects house prices. When it comes to the structure of Canada's population, I find our country to be fascinating. I spend a good chunk of my time studying real estate markets, in Canada and around the world, looking at where population is concentrated, how cities are set up, and how those factors influence property prices. When I travel to other parts of the world to talk to real estate investors about Canadian real estate, one of my favourite things to do is tell investors who don't know a lot about Canada how incredibly concentrated our population is. The responses can be priceless.

I've found that people who have never been here or don't know much about the country usually do know three things. The first is that Canada is the second-largest country in the world by area. The second is that our population of 36 million people is pretty small.

With more than 9 million square kilometres of land, that works out to about 3.4 people per square kilometre. About 167 Canadian football fields fit into a square kilometre (CFL fields are 43-percent larger than NFL fields — just saying), which means Canadians have about forty-nine football fields of space each. That's a lot of space for each of us to run around in.

Canada's population starts to look very, very small when you compare it to the United States, which has a population of 332 million people. The United States is slightly smaller than Canada by area and has more than nine times as

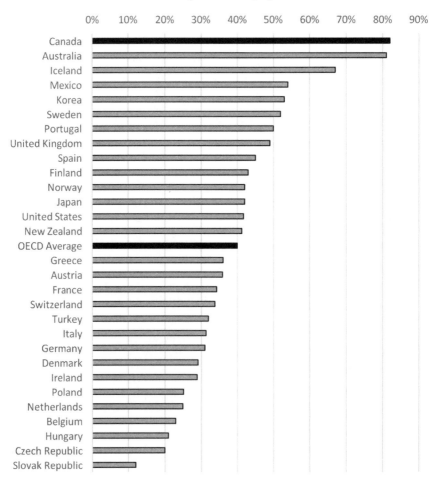

## OECD Index Of Geographic Concentration Of Population (%)

Source: OECD Regions at a Glance.

many people, leaving about thirty-five people per square kilometre. That's less than five Canadian football fields for each American. Not cramped, but we still have ten times as much space each as of our friends south of the border.

But even the United States is pretty spread out when compared to other countries. India, at almost 1.3 billion people, has about thirty-five times the population of Canada and a land area of about one-third the size of Canada, with almost 390 people per square kilometre. That's less than a half a football field each. With 160 million people, Bangladesh is tops among large countries, with almost seven people per football field.

It's easy to see why outsiders looking in at Canada might think it's a vast, barren land, one that is barely populated. Maybe they think all Canadians live solitary lives in cabins deep in the woods, rarely running into each other. After all, each of us has almost fifty football fields of space, while the average Bangladeshi shares a single field with six friends.

Which brings us to the third thing most people know about Canada: It gets cold. For a good chunk of the year. In fact, in winter Canada is one of the coldest places in the world — almost as cold as Russia, and not much warmer than Antarctica

Why does this matter? For all of Canada's massive expanses of land, Canadians are living virtually on top of each other.

Canadians are overwhelmingly concentrated in just a few cities across the country, with more than 80 percent of Canadians living within 160 kilometres of the U.S. border. Any further north, and it starts to get very cold.

> Canadians are overwhelmingly concentrated in just a few cities across the country.

All joking aside, the population centres are also concentrated along the border because a large portion of the border runs along the St. Lawrence River and the Great Lakes, which are important shipping and trade routes and were even more important over 100 years ago when Canada's largest cities were beginning to establish themselves as major population centres. Even today, the vast majority of Canada's trade is with the United States, providing economic incentive for population centres to be close to the border.

Overall, some 55 percent of Canadians live in the ten largest cities in Canada. That's twice the share of Americans in the U.S.'s largest cities.

| Census Metropolitan Area | Population | % of Population |
|---|---|---|
| Toronto | 6,129,934 | 17% |
| Montreal | 4,060,692 | 11% |
| Vancouver | 2,504,340 | 7% |
| Calgary | 1,439,756 | 4% |
| Edmonton | 1,363,277 | 4% |
| Ottawa | 1,332,001 | 4% |
| Quebec | 806,359 | 2% |
| Winnipeg | 793,428 | 2% |
| Hamilton | 771,703 | 2% |
| Kitchener-Cambridge-Waterloo | 511,319 | 1% |
| Top 10 CMAs | 19,712,809 | 55% |
| Canada | 35,985,751 | 100% |

Source: Statistics Canada, 2015.

| Metropolitan Statistical Area | Population | % of Population |
|---|---|---|
| New York | 20,182,305 | 6% |
| Los Angeles | 13,340,068 | 4% |
| Chicago | 9,551,031 | 3% |
| Dallas | 7,102,796 | 2% |
| Houston | 6,656,947 | 2% |
| Washington, D.C. | 6,097,684 | 2% |
| Philadelphia | 6,069,875 | 2% |
| Miami | 6,012,331 | 2% |
| Atlanta | 5,710,795 | 2% |
| Boston | 4,774,321 | 1% |
| Top 10 CMAs | 85,498,153 | 27% |
| United States | 321,418,820 | 100% |

Source: U.S. Census Bureau, 2015.

The fact that so many of us live in just a handful of places means we generally live in big cities. Populations globally are increasingly moving into cities. So, while in theory we each have an enormous amount of space, when it comes to the housing market, Canadians choose to live big-city lives: Canada is a highly urban country.

Should we be surprised house prices in Canada are high when we all live in big cities? I don't think so.

However, knowing some of the reasons Canadian house prices have risen doesn't change the fact that housing here is expensive. So expensive that it's gotten a lot of very smart people very concerned.

# CHAPTER 6

## What Really Drives Real Estate Prices — The Golden Rule

If we're going to be talking about the benefits of renting versus buying, we have to talk about why house prices rise and fall. It's unavoidable! The price of real estate has an impact on the cost of renting, but it has an even larger impact on the cost of home ownership. Even more important, the popularity of home ownership is highly dependent upon the broad-based belief and expectation that house prices will go up.

Before we go any further, let me say that, as a general rule, in this book when I talk about houses and homes, I'm referring to all formats of housing: apartments, townhouses, semi-detached, single-family, and any other iteration of housing out there. All housing is priced based on the same group of factors, as we're about to explore.

Of course, we all collectively have many discussions about housing, with friends, family, real estate agents, strangers, and co-workers. However, it is remarkable how few of those discussions focus on what makes houses go up or down in value. We have lots of conversations about *how much* our houses have gone up or down and what that means for our personal wealth, but not why they go up.

These conversations sometimes touch on topics that have some impact. Interest rates affect how much of a mortgage payment you can afford. Income growth is another topic that has something to do with house prices. Sometimes you'll hear about new highways or new subways nearby that make transit better. That usually helps a house price.

The few conversations we do have about what drives house prices are usually short, at least in part because there are no clear answers and there are many factors at play. Is it population growth that drives house prices? What about inflation? Do houses always only go up in value, like many people say? The truth is that different houses go up and down for different reasons. Some houses go up, some go up a lot, and some go down.

We're going to talk about some simple ways to think about houses that will give you a better chance at understanding how house prices will change over time, and also help explain how prices got to where they are today.

> House prices are driven by supply and demand. Everything else you hear about what drives house prices is about something that affects supply or demand.

The most complete and true statement that anyone can make on the topic is that house prices are driven by supply and demand. Just like everything else in the world, if there are more people who want a product than there are of that product, the price will rise. If there is more of that product than there are people who want that product, then the price will fall. It's that simple. Everything else you hear about what drives house prices is about something that is affecting either supply or demand for housing.

We'll cover a number of things that can affect house prices, and every one of them is a factor that affects either supply of housing or demand for housing. We'll also look at which ones are most important and how to figure out how each looks for a given property. But first, the Golden Rule.

Over the many years I've been analyzing real estate, I've come up with a simple rule that helps me understand how a given property's value might change over time. I use it when I analyze office buildings, shopping centres, industrial warehouses, apartment buildings, self-storage properties, houses, and generally any real estate investment a person or company can make. Here goes.

## THE GOLDEN RULE OF REAL ESTATE (PART 1 OF 2)

**Buildings never go up in value. Ever. Period.**

Pretty simple, no?

That statement is true of all types of buildings, including houses. If you can accept that as a universal truth, you're a lot closer to understanding property value than most people ever get.

But Alex, have Canadian house prices risen at an average of almost 5 percent a year for the last twenty-five years?

Yes, they did. But we didn't talk about why.

The trick here is that you generally don't just buy a house — you buy the house *and* the land that it sits on. The actual house goes down in value in *real* terms. Always. Without any exceptions.

That's because, as a house gets older, it wears out. The roof gets older and maybe it starts to leak. The furnace gets older and needs repairs. The kitchen starts to look older, a little bit worn, and maybe the colours go out of style. The counters wear out. The fridge dies. Even the floors eventually weaken and begin to fail. Detached home, townhouse, high-rise — parts of every home wear out over time.

Virtually every element of a house gradually fails. That is why there are maintenance costs. If we do a great job of maintaining a house, by keeping on top of regular maintenance items and servicing all the various elements of a house, we can slow down the pace at which the house goes down in value. But there is a cost to maintaining a house, and those costs don't increase the value of a house, they maintain it.

If buildings go down in value, how have home prices risen?

## THE GOLDEN RULE OF REAL ESTATE (PART 2 OF 2)

**Only land can go up in value.**

Some land goes up a little, and some goes up a lot. Sometimes the land goes down in value. But the house always goes down in value. Both parts of this rule are important to keep in mind when considering "investing" in a home and when comparing the potential financial benefits of doing so compared to the cost of renting.

This rule I've created helps me to gain perspective when I'm trying to value real estate. I created the rule based on a few things I kept noticing as I was making my way into the real estate industry:

1.  All properties have maintenance costs.
2.  For tax purposes, properties are depreciated — a fixed percentage of a property's purchase price can be expensed each year against income the property generates.
3.  Properties in large cities tend to perform better than rural properties over time.

What the first two observations told me was that buildings go down in value, while the third observation told me that, where land is scarce, property values can go up. And, conversely, where land isn't scarce, its value doesn't tend to go up.

I like to think that I created this rule, but that might be an overstatement. I think it would be more accurate to say I rediscovered a rule that has been around ever since real estate has been around: The three most important things in real estate are Location, Location, and Location.

I just might have explained it a little better.

When I first got into the real estate industry, I had heard "Location, Location, Location" a few times, as you might have, and I asked a few people what that meant. Each person answered in a different way, which told me that it meant different things to different people. The most common theme I heard in the answers was that location wasn't just the most important aspect of investing in real estate; it was far and away the most important. That why it was the first, second, and third most important things.

I usually asked a follow-up question or two, like, "What makes a good location?" or "Why is location the most important thing?"

That's where the common threads in the answers started to break down. The answers to the follow-up questions ranged from cryptic riddles to honest admissions, such as that it's hard to describe a good location — "you can just tell" — to things like proximity to transit, and many other suggestions. The truth is that a good location means different things to different people, and different things for different uses. A good location for an industrial building — close to an airport, rail line, and major highway — is a bad location for a house. A good location for a suburban shopping centre — near lots of suburban homes so it's easy for people to get there from home — doesn't make for a good location for an office building.

I found it hard to understand why nobody could give me a good, complete answer to the question of what makes a good location, or why location was the most important thing. It just was. Never quite satisfied by the answers I'd received, I thought about "Location, Location, Location" from time to time as I learned more about real estate.

As I spent more and more time analyzing real estate, I realized that location was the defining feature of land. A property could have a lot of other defining characteristics: type of building (retail or office, for instance); size of building; age of building; state of repair of building; or even land area. But when it comes to trying to figure out what is going to happen to the value of a real estate investment over the long-term (which is much easier than figuring out what is going to happen in the short-term), nothing is more important than location.

> Location — the defining feature of land — dictates how house prices will change over time.

Putting that together with my Golden Rule of Real Estate, it becomes clearer what drives house prices: the land and its defining feature, location. Location dictates how value will change over time. That's what people mean when they say, "Location, Location, Location." Even if they themselves can't tell you clearly what the phrase means.

Now we can use that information to make better housing decisions.

We still haven't answered the question of what a good location is. Let's dig into that topic. If supply and demand drive house prices, we need to look at what factors drive demand for housing, and how supply responds to demand.

# CHAPTER 7

## What Really Drives Real Estate Prices — Demand for Housing

### POPULATION AND GROWTH

Demand. This is the harder to figure out half of the supply and demand dynamic that drives house prices. I think that's because we humans do strange and unpredictable things, and because there are many things that can influence behaviour and decision making. To tackle the questions of what drives demand, we'll start with the most basic driver of demand: people.

People live in houses. The more people there are, the more houses are needed. Population growth is the single biggest driver of demand for housing, and positive growth is a critical feature of any healthy housing market.

When a population is declining, it needs fewer houses. But houses don't just disappear, so less population leaves extra houses available. When there is more of a product than there is demand, prices will fall.

When a population is growing, it needs more houses. If there's more demand than there are houses, prices will rise in response. That goes for rental and owned — prices include both the price needed to buy the home and the rent needed to rent the home.

Another old industry saying is that all real estate is a local business. It can be interpreted in many ways. Tying it back to "Location, Location, Location," to say real estate is a local business is to say that what is happening in the immediate area of the property is what is most important.

From a population growth perspective, that means that, while having national population growth is good, it's more important to have provincial population growth. Even more important is to have population growth in the city, and still more important is to have population growth in the neighbourhood where a property is located.

Population growth can be driven by many different things. It's pretty easy to figure out what those things are. Just think of things that would make you want to live somewhere.

If you're twenty-four years old, you probably want to live somewhere that is convenient: near public transit, close to friends and work. You'll want a good job. Maybe you enjoy a vibrant nightlife. That could mean Liberty Village in Toronto, Yaletown in Vancouver, Griffintown in Montreal, ByWard Market in Ottawa, Ritchie in Edmonton, or Eau Claire in Calgary.

What is particularly great about a lot of these neighbourhoods is that they offer a good mix of rental and owned homes to live in, including a lot of high-rise homes. When you're in your twenties, there's a lot of change going on in your life, and you generally have a lot of free time to enjoy all of the amazing things to do in these vibrant neighbourhoods.

If you're in your thirties or forties, you may have children, and if so, you'll probably want to live near great schools and clean and safe parks. You still want to be close to transit and good jobs. You might want more space in your house (for more people) and even a backyard.

You'll find great neighbourhoods with these characteristics all over Canadian cities. Generally speaking, the farther you get from public transit, the more difficult it is to find rental housing. That means it could get more difficult to find a broad range of rental homes in some of these neighbourhoods, but if you keep close to transit and spend a bit more time looking for the right rental, you'll find it.

If you're in your sixties or seventies, you probably want to live close to friends and family (maybe near grandkids!), nice restaurants and theatres, and good transit. Being close to employment might become less of a priority if you're retired or working part-time. These characteristics (including excellent transit) can be found in many neighbourhoods, which means that there are lots of options for both the renter and the owner.

Whatever priorities you would put at the top of your list, most people would agree that being close to good jobs would be on there, as would being close to transit or good roads, so they can get around, and close to entertainment.

Of course, everyone would like to live in the best location, with a large, beautiful house on a large, beautiful property that is close to jobs, transit, and entertainment. The more appealing a place is, the more likely you are to find population growth.

Among all of these factors, the single most important driver of population growth is proximity to good jobs. You'll find the fastest growing populations where there are lots of jobs.

## TRANSPORTATION AND TRANSIT

If you own a plot of land, it's always in exactly the same location. You might be able to move the house that sits on the land, but that's extremely rare and very expensive. Let's just agree that when you buy a house, it will always be where it is.

Your ability to get to and from that piece of land is something that definitely has an impact on how much that house is worth. There's a cost to commuting, and commuting takes time. Whether it's to and from a job, to and from friends and family, or to and from entertainment and other services, like your doctor's office or the barber shop or the grocery store, it takes time and energy to move from one place to another.

When you look at house prices, you'll find that houses close to all of the kinds of things people need in their lives are more expensive than those that are farther away. You'll find that suburban homes are usually less expensive than inner-city homes (in cities with clean, safe cores). That reflects the extra costs associated with getting to and from the city centre, where there is an abundance of services; a large, concentrated population; and lots of jobs.

It makes sense: People should be willing to pay more for a house in a location where they can walk across the street to work and a block over for groceries, and where they can visit friends, family, entertainment, and every other service they want without getting into a car. The time saved through that convenience has to be worth something, never mind the savings of not having a car and the cost of gas and insurance.

That might be an extreme case — most people end up having cars, and most people have a longer commute to work than walking across the street — but the principle remains the same. If you have a house that is half the drive time from all of these things, you should be willing to pay more for it than a house that is twice as far.

Just like population growth, the most important factor in transportation is the ability to get from your home to your place of work. After all, the place most of us go the most often is work — usually five or so return trips a week!

Bringing this back to the Golden Rule, transportation has an almost magical power that can actually alter location. Because of this power, transportation holds a special place in the world of house prices.

You buy a house and it will always be in exactly the same place as it was the day you bought it. The place you work will always be in the exact same place as it was the day you started. The only ways to change these two realities are to move to another house, to change jobs, or to have your company move its location. But there's something else interesting that can happen to change the distance between these two places, without either place moving an inch: transportation.

In 1980, my family moved to the eastern suburbs of Toronto from a house centrally located in the city. My sister and I were young, and I imagine my parents wanted all the things that typically draw families out to the suburbs: a bigger house, with more space for kids and all the junk they bring with them, as well as a bigger yard and more places for the kids to play safely. The suburbs are usually a little quieter, with wider sidewalks and boulevards, and safer for untethered children.

> Transportation has an almost magical power that can actually alter location.

At the time my father worked in the downtown core, on Yonge Street, and our new home was near Port Union Road and Lawrence Avenue. The distance between our home and my father's office was just under twenty-five kilometres. By highway, it was closer to forty kilometres. Either way, it took my dad about twenty-five minutes to drive to work.

In the 1980s, Toronto was growing fast, and that growth was mostly at the perimeter. Suburbs were rapidly sprawling outward in all directions, filled with the wide streets, large homes, and big backyards that the baby boom generation was craving, with millions of boomers having just started families.

What happened next was amazing. Our house gradually got farther and farther away from my dad's office. It happened one day at a time, one car at a time. Street after street of suburb was built, and the highways and roads became gradually busier and busier.

My parents moved back downtown in 1999, just prior to my father retiring. By the time they left West Hill, as our neighbourhood was known, the commute my father made to work had increased from the twenty-five minutes it took when we moved there in 1980 to an hour and twenty minutes. In the nineteen years we lived there, my father's commute more than tripled, despite the distance not changing an inch. That's the power of transportation.

Now, Toronto's population grew remarkably over that period. More rapidly than any other major city in Canada, despite being the largest to begin with, at a pace of slightly over 2 percent per year, for total growth of 45 percent (according to City of Toronto Urban Development Services). While there have been many critics of the city's public transit planning foresight, growing so quickly makes it difficult to keep up with transit infrastructure, which is expensive and requires very long lead times to develop.

Nevertheless, Toronto has become a lot more congested over the past few decades, and it continues to get more congested as the population continues to grow at a rapid pace — particularly rapid for such a large city. That means things have been getting farther and farther apart, which has meant that demand for homes in peripheral locations has been impact by congestion costs over time.

Transportation can, however, also bring places closer together. New highways, subways, HOV lanes, rapid transit, and other forms of mass transit tend to reduce commute times, improving the locations of properties over time.

While Toronto has continued to get more and more congested, some neighbourhoods have seen significant transportation and accessibility improvements as major infrastructure projects have progressed. A new highway, the 407 private express toll road across the northern edge of the city, opened less than ten kilometres north of the city's main east–west expressway, the 401. But highways aren't the way to really improve transportation in large cities, and they don't tend to have the biggest impacts on property values. They have more impact on house prices in satellite suburbs, but not within a city.

That honour usually goes to subways. Subways typically run under cities that have already been built up, and when new subways open, they create brand-new passenger capacity with close to zero related traffic congestion and very reliable travel times. Absent new subway lines (or very well-executed light rail), there is little hope of changing local traffic for the better in urban locations. So, unless a subway is expected soon, it's reasonable to expect local traffic congestion will get worse over time, as a city continues to grow.

When a new subway line does arrive, it can have a dramatic impact on local house prices. That's because the transportation available for homeowners to travel to and away from their homes improves significantly. Even the road congestion eases as more former drivers take advantage of the affordable, reliable, and fast subway option.

As with everything else with house prices, nailing down a precise impact on prices from a subway line opening nearby is impossible. There have been lots of studies completed, but each is usually focused on a specific new subway, and it's very difficult to control for other factors. Of the research studies I've read, the most common estimate is a 10- to 20-percent increase to local house prices, compared to homes farther away from the subway. But these seem more like guesses than statistically proven facts. I'm more comfortable saying that it's quite a nice positive, and that, over time, the 10- to 20-percent figure might prove conservative.

Absent any improvements to transportation infrastructure, like subways or highways, if a city is growing its population, traffic and congestion should have a slightly negative impact on the prices of houses most exposed to long and growing commutes — those generally out at the perimeter of the city. Conversely, it should have a relatively positive impact on particularly well-located properties, those generally very close to employment hubs.

## INTEREST RATES

Part of the cost of buying houses for most homeowners is the mortgage payment. It is made up of both principal and interest. If you assume each homebuyer has a certain income and that they are willing to spend only a certain percentage of their income on a mortgage payment, then you can calculate the maximum mortgage payment they can afford to pay each month. The level of the interest rate determines how much interest expense is required in each mortgage payment. The lower the interest rate, the more money the homebuyer can pay for a home at the same monthly mortgage

One thing is clear: Lower interest rates put upward pressure on house prices, but not on rents.

payment. The lower the interest rate, the lower the interest expense portion of the mortgage payment, and the higher the principal portion of the payment.

In a sense, interest rates are the cost of money. The cheaper money is, the less money homebuyers need to spend on borrowing money and the more they can spend on the actual house.

It makes sense. Unfortunately, it's not entirely clear what exactly that relationship actually translates into, in mathematical terms. In fact, none of the factors we're discussing here can be boiled down to a rule about how much of an impact any of them have on house prices.

One thing about the effect of interest rates on housing is clear: Lower interest rates put upward pressure on house prices, but not on rents. The exceptionally low interest rates currently available in Canada have undoubtedly driven house prices higher, but they have not driven rents higher. Low interest rates are a strong sign that it's a good time to rent.

## FOREIGNERS, SPECULATORS, AND EXCHANGE STUDENTS

There's been an awful lot of speculation and debate about the role of investors, and particularly foreign investors, in Canadian housing markets. There isn't a lot of information available about how significant a factor speculative investors, foreign investors, or other investors might be in the housing market, partly because it's very difficult to define what constitutes an investor versus a normal homebuyer.

Is an investor a person who buys a property and never intends to occupy the unit? Maybe. What if they only stay at the property for one week a year? How about if it is bought to rent out to a tenant? Probably. What about if the tenant they rent the house to is a relative? What if it's their child? Does it matter if the child is just living in the property while completing a degree, or if they plan to stay after finishing school?

How about foreign buyers? Is a foreigner a person who has a principal residence in a foreign country, where they spend most of their time? Is it their last name or the language they speak that makes them a foreigner?

No matter how you define a speculator, investor, or foreign buyer, it's certain that they all represent added demand in a housing market, and their presence can contribute toward higher prices.

The attention paid to the topic of speculators and foreign investors naturally rises as housing becomes more and more expensive. The debate about foreign investors and speculators is most acute in Vancouver, Canada's most expensive market and a city where 40 percent of the total population was born outside Canada. Vancouver has not only seen strong immigration volumes, but it has included a specific type of immigrant: immigrant investors. Canada's federal government immigrant investor program, and its similar immigrant entrepreneur program, offered the opportunity for wealthy foreigners to immigrate to Canada on a fast-tracked basis and with fewer requirements, like language skills, than other immigrants. The program was in place from 1986 until 2014 and required a specific minimum net worth ($1.6 million in its final years) and an investment "in Canada" ($800,000 was the last minimum) for a set period of time. The investment was made in the form of a loan to the government of Canada, bearing no interest for a period of five years (shorter earlier in the program), which was then invested into the economy through a variety of means, and returned to the immigrant at the end of five years.

The program was cancelled in 2014 amid complaints that it was being abused, with reports that many participants were using the program to first gain permanent resident status, and then Canadian citizenship, only to then return to their homes abroad to run businesses, leaving their spouses and children to live in Canada and, particularly, in Vancouver. For very wealthy foreigners, the program offered a convenient and affordable type of insurance in the form of a second citizenship status, as well as a very attractive location for family members to live if political unrest or deteriorating business conditions forced these program participants to leave their home country.

It's possible some immigrant investors remained in Canada long enough to obtain citizenship, only to return to their original countries while continuing to own homes in Vancouver and leaving them vacant aside from occasional visits. There has been speculation that spouses and children have remained living in Canada while the investor has continued working abroad, which suggests their families might not be fully participating in the economy by generating employment income and paying taxes. Whether their homes are vacant or are occupied by unemployed spouses and children, the individuals who have benefitted from the immigrant investor program seem to have been strong contributors to the meteoric rise of house prices in Vancouver, particularly for high-end homes, reaching into the multi-million-dollar range.

While the federal government's immigrant investor program was cancelled in 2014, the province of Quebec has continued to operate a parallel but smaller program, with the requirement that participants have the intent of settling in the province upon moving to Canada. There is limited information available on where participants in the program end up living.

Similar concerns about foreign investors and speculators have become more common in Toronto recently, as house prices in the city have continued to rise. First it was the city's unrelenting condo boom, which has continued for more than a decade, adding well more than a hundred thousand units to the city's downtown core alone. As single-family house prices have continued to rise, reports of foreign investors participating in that market have risen too.

As a guy who analyzes investment in real estate for a living, I find the role of foreign investors and speculators interesting and complicated. On the one hand, there's nothing inherently wrong with investors buying homes as investments. Every homeowner in the world is part investor, though most are more motivated by solving the problem of where to live and keep all their possessions. On the other hand, speculative investment activity can distort markets, create bubbles, and interfere with the underlying market — in this case, housing.

> While speculative investing can drive up both house prices and rents, the downside risk of a collapse is really only a problem for homeowners.

If speculators created a huge bubble in the Canadian coffee market and prices were to rise to outrageous levels, most Canadians would either stop drinking coffee, switch to drinking tea or caffeinated sodas, or just grudgingly pay the high prices for coffee and cut some other expenses in their budgets to offset the increased coffee budget. But when it comes to housing, it's not a minor budget item for most people: It's their single largest expense, whether they buy or rent. And it's not an optional expense. Housing is one of the most basic needs of Canadians.

With housing such a critical part of our lives, and also the largest asset of most Canadian homeowners, too much speculative investment can create real problems for Canadians and the Canadian housing market.

With too much investor demand for any type of investment, prices will rise. Fortunately, when it comes to the housing market, there are actually two markets: the rental market and the ownership market. The difficult-to-measure but potentially significant role of foreign and speculative investors in some Canadian housing markets is really concentrated in the ownership side. While speculative investing can drive up both house prices and rents, making it difficult to afford housing, the downside risk of a collapse in the event investors begin to flee our housing market is really only a problem for homeowners. Particularly homeowners with mortgages, for whom the house price could drop below the mortgage owed. Renters would merely begin to see the benefits of the lower rents. One more good reason to consider renting!

## INCOME AND INCOME GROWTH

Income and income growth are important factors in house prices. Homes are big, expensive purchases, and they're usually bought using a mortgage. The more income and the more income growth there is in a city, the more capacity the population has to make higher mortgage payments and pay higher prices for the housing in the city. But what is interesting about income and income growth is that, although high incomes provide the capacity for the population to pay a higher price for homes, they don't necessarily cause prices to go higher. Provided new homes can be built in the market, demand remains balanced with supply. Looking at Canada's markets, if incomes drove house prices, one might expect Calgary and Edmonton, with the highest and second-highest average household income among large Canadian cities, to have the highest house prices. But they don't, because in both cities there have been lots and lots of new homes built over the last decade. This tells us that a lack of income and income growth can limit house prices, but a high income and rapid income growth don't drive house prices higher on their own.

Often, rapidly growing single industries create boom towns, where the most extreme examples of population growth occur, driven by an abundance of good-paying jobs and resulting in rapid house price growth. These markets can be dangerous, with short-term imbalances creating booms and busts. High and rising incomes make it possible for house prices to increase rapidly, and booming population growth can drive surging demand.

Las Vegas was one such place this occurred, in the years leading up to the 2007–2009 U.S. housing crash. Population growth in Las Vegas was an astounding 3.5 percent per year in the years between 2000 and 2010, making it the fastest-growing major city in the United States over that period. By comparison, the U.S. population grew by slightly less than 1 percent per year over the same period.

House prices in Las Vegas surged 135 percent between 2000 and the peak in 2006, sharply ahead of the 58-percent average increase seen across the eleven cities tracked by the Case-Shiller house price index, as construction of new homes struggled to keep pace with the remarkable population growth.

When the U.S. housing crash hit, beginning in late 2006, Las Vegas house prices fell, by the end of 2011, 62 percent from their peak. This massive crash was substantially more than the 39-percent average across the eleven cities.

This is where the supply side comes in, along with the Golden Rule.

# CHAPTER 8

## What Really Drives Real Estate Prices — Supply of Housing

You can't know anything about where house prices might go by understanding just demand or by understanding just supply. You need both. It's not simply enough to know how quickly the population is growing or how many houses have been built or are going to be built. You need to know both supply and demand to see where house prices might be headed.

Between the two, I've found supply to be the easier one to understand and the one that is more helpful in figuring out the long-term prospects for house prices. Over a short period of a couple years, strong demand growth can lead to a shortage of the materials and labour required to build new houses, which can cause house prices to go up. But there are rarely any significant or sustained limits on the supply of materials and labour. If the house prices are high enough to cover the cost of new buildings, construction of new homes will follow, helping restore the balance between supply and demand and bringing house prices back down.

## THE DEVELOPMENT PROCESS

However, housing takes a long time to build. Not just the actual building, but all of the steps that take place before it's built. First you need to get municipal zoning approval for the type of housing you'd like to build, and then all of the services need to be developed — sewers, water supply, power, and roads, among others. Designs, blueprints and technical plans need to be completed. Permits for construction must then be obtained. All of that is before the construction begins, which can last up to a year for single-family or low-rise homes and as long as long as three or more years for high-rise construction. Depending on how difficult it is to obtain approvals for new developments and how long the process takes, the supply of housing can be limited by the regulatory process of securing zoning, permits, and other approvals for construction. For instance, in Toronto the entire process of creating new housing can take more than ten years today.

In some places there are policy constraints that limit the types of housing and other buildings that are allowed to be built. Whitehorse, in the Yukon, limits all buildings to no more than four storeys due to a nearby geological fault line and fears of earthquakes that could bring down taller buildings. In Washington, D.C., no building may be taller than twenty feet higher than the width of the road it is on, and in any event is limited to a specific height depending on the type of building. Washington's height restrictions date back to 1899, when they reflected concerns about the whether it was safe to build buildings much taller than one hundred feet, with the relatively new innovations in steel construction, and also the limitations of the fire department in fighting fires more than a couple floors up. These examples relate to height, but many places have restrictions on lot sizes, construction materials, engineering standards, and numerous other limitations.

Rules and regulations like these, along with sometimes onerous zoning and permitting processes, can have a significant impact on the amount of new housing that can be built in response to rising demand in a given period.

The long lead time of zoning approvals also makes it easier to see the supply outlook over the next few years, but even easier to see than that is the longer-term supply outlook, which can have even more of an impact. And it boils down to one thing: land.

## LAND

The supply of land provides the ultimate constraint on housing supply, and it can be one of the biggest drivers of housing prices. Provided a market has a positive population growth outlook, the availability of land on which to build more housing should play a critical role in house prices over the long term.

Let's consider what happens when a city sees jobs growth and population growth and demand for housing rises. As house prices rise, it becomes more attractive for home builders to build new homes. If there is ample available land at low prices, the cost of building new houses will be the sum of the cost of the materials and labour required to build those houses and the small portion related to the cost of the land.

Las Vegas was a prime example of this kind of market in the early 2000s, with essentially no limit to the amount of land available on which to build. As the broader U.S. housing boom picked up, in part due to aggressive pro-home ownership housing policy, Las Vegas boomed. As it did, lots of jobs were created, including jobs building houses. This drew even more people to Vegas for the jobs, driving even more demand for housing. As house prices rose, new house construction rose. The temporary limitations of the housing industry to respond to the rising demand led to a rapid rate of growth in house prices, as builders struggled to find the materials and labour to build houses fast enough to keep up with demand.

Ultimately, the housing market crashed, since there was no limit to the supply of housing. No matter how many people moved there, they could always build more housing. It just took a little longer than people were willing to wait.

The run-up in house prices in Las Vegas violated the Golden Rule of Real Estate: Only the land can go up in value, not the building. The rapid growth in prices related to the buildings, not the land. With an essentially unlimited supply of land, it didn't matter how many people moved to Las Vegas; there would ultimately be more than enough land. There was no reason for land prices to go up.

Now let's look at housing markets where there is a real constraint on land supply, like New York City. As the population grows and employment grows, house prices rise. Unlike Las Vegas, New York doesn't have an unlimited amount of land to build on. In fact, land is quite scarce, and, as a result, the land portion of the value of a home is quite high. In order to build more housing, developers need to buy existing buildings, which can be quite expensive, and tear them down, and they are forced to build higher-density housing (more people per square foot of land) — low-rise apartments instead of single-family homes, or high-rise buildings instead of low-rise.

Not only is the land more expensive, but the cost of building higher-density housing is more expensive on a per-square-foot basis than low-density housing. This is particularly true of tall high-rise housing, for which the prices rise as the buildings get taller and taller.

As the cost of adding new supply to the housing market rises, so does the price of existing housing. And another interesting thing happens. In a land-constrained market, single-family and low-rise house prices can rise at a faster rate than incomes, sometimes significantly, and do so on a sustained basis. The key here is that, with a fixed supply of land in a city with a growing population, the portion of the population that owns the fixed number of low-density homes falls as a percentage of the total population.

Sometimes referred to as the exclusion effect, what happens is that the average incomes and wealth of the buyers of those homes rises, even if overall incomes and wealth aren't rising. Imagine a fixed number of single-family homes in a market at one point was owned by the wealthiest 25 percent of the population. Over time, as the population grew and more apartment-style housing was built, the number of single-family homeowners declines as a percentage of the now-larger population, coming to represent just 20 percent of the total population. The top 20 percent of incomes are higher than the top 25 percent of incomes, as the lowest incomes among the top 25 percent are not included in the top 20 percent of incomes.

But the impact of land constraints doesn't end there. Comparing the population growth rates of Las Vegas and New York shows that, even during the boom years, New York was growing at a significantly slower rate than Las Vegas. This is because Las Vegas had the ability to accommodate significant population growth at a relatively low cost, while New York didn't.

When housing markets crash, it's typically because there is a combination of supply and demand changes that lead to demand falling below supply. Using Las Vegas and New York as examples, the appeal of land-constrained markets is that the supply of land is fixed, while the demand growth tends to be lower. The crash witnessed in Las Vegas was a combination of high levels of new construction with a collapse in demand.

While land-constrained markets can see significant declines in demand, they are structurally limited in terms of how much new supply can be delivered. This tends to make land-constrained markets both more expensive and also less subject to price volatility.

The most expensive housing markets in the world, and most consistently expensive, all have significant land constraints. New York, Hong

Kong, London, and San Francisco are all cities that have consistently topped the list of the most expensive cities in the world, and all have significant land constraints.

New York includes five boroughs: Queens and Brooklyn, which are both on the southwestern tip of Long Island; the Bronx, which sits on the southern tip of a peninsula bordered by the Hudson River, the Harlem River, and the East River; and Staten Island. Sitting at the centre is the most expensive housing market of the five boroughs, the island of Manhattan.

Hong Kong is a series of islands, including the island of Hong Kong, as well as a small peninsula bordered by water on three sides and the Chinese border to the north. The most expensive housing in Hong Kong is on Hong Kong Island.

London has the most expensive housing of any major city in Europe. London clearly isn't an island, but it does have other land constraints. These include a very large greenbelt (an area legally protected from being developed; typically undeveloped natural land or agricultural land), as well as "protected views" that prevent large buildings from being built that would obstruct views between notable locations across the city, including St. Paul's Cathedral and the Palace of Westminster (the United Kingdom's House of Commons).

Land constraints don't guarantee high or stable house prices, but they do tend to make understanding a housing market a little easier because one half of the supply and demand dynamic is well understood.

◉　◉　◉

So how can we figure out if house prices are likely to go up or down? It is extremely difficult, and, truthfully, the best we can do is identify factors that are likely to contribute to house price moments in the future. If it were easier than that, there wouldn't be so much debate about the topic.

What we can now do is look at Canada's biggest cities and figure out what kinds of markets they are: New Yorks or Las Vegases?

# CHAPTER 9
## The Big Six

Canada's housing markets include some New Yorks and some Las Vegases. We have some very expensive markets and some less expensive markets. To better understand Canada's housing market, we'll look at Canada's six largest markets to learn about how they stack up and why different markets are more and less expensive. We'll also look at the appeal of renting in each of these markets.

For each city, we'll look at population trends, employment profiles, and the physical structure of the markets, and we'll compare house prices to incomes and to rents to understand how renting compares to owning in each market.

Comparing the average price of a home to the average income provides a measure of how costly houses are in different markets, where incomes are different. Historically, in periods of more normal interest rates (significantly higher than they are today), house prices across most markets have ranged from three to five times gross average income. In major cities with significant land constraints, price to income can range from five times to as much as twelve times or more. Very low interest rates tend to push these averages up. Dividing average house prices by average annual rent shows how growth in house prices and growth in rents compare over time and how expensive owning is compared to renting.

After reading this chapter, it should be clear that Canadian house prices are high compared to historical levels, that renting has remained quite affordable, and that some cities are more affordable than others for both renting and owning.

Let's start with Toronto.

## TORONTO

The Toronto Census Metropolitan Area (CMA) is the largest city in Canada by a wide margin. With a population of 6.1 million, Toronto is more than 50 percent larger than Canada's second-largest metropolitan area, Montreal. Not only is it large, but it's also consistently growing quickly, particularly for such a large city, averaging 1.6 percent per year over the past decade.

Toronto is the number one destination for immigrants in Canada, powering its unusually high growth rate for such a large city. Toronto's population is 46 percent immigrant, including 7 percent considered recent (having immigrated to Canada in the past five years), putting the city significantly ahead of all other Canadian cities (Vancouver is closest at 40 percent) in terms of immigrant share of the population.

Canada's pro-immigration policies and broad-based public support for multiculturalism and immigration has made Toronto one of the most ethnically diverse large cities in the world. (And one of the greatest in the world, if you ask me!)

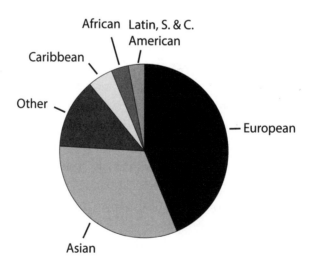

### Toronto's Ethnicity

Source: Statistics Canada, 2011.

Toronto also has quite a diverse economy, spanning government, financial services, healthcare, education, and many other industries. Notably, employment in natural resources fields is less than 0.3 percent of Toronto's employment.

## Toronto Employment

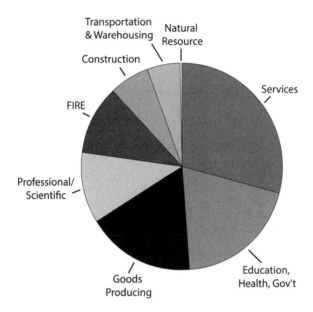

(FIRE stands for Finance, Insurance, and Real Estate.)
Source: Statistics Canada, 2011.

Queen's Park, the home of the Ontario provincial government, is less than two kilometres from Toronto City Hall, with both located in the heart of downtown. As is the Central Business District (CBD), the centre of Toronto's financial services industry and home to over 85 million square feet of Canada's office buildings. Five of Canada's "big six" banks are headquartered in Toronto, as are both of Canada's largest insurance companies, along with Canada's largest stock exchange and the vast majority of Canada's brokerages. Clustered on University Avenue, but also scattered through the city, are more than a dozen major hospitals and more than a dozen smaller hospitals. University Avenue is home to one of the largest clusters of medical research organizations in the world. The city also has eight universities and colleges.

In short, the city is rapidly growing, with a broadly diversified economy. What's more, the city has been very consistently growing for a long, long time. The growth of the city included a significant amount of apartment construction in the late 1960s and 1970s, followed by a pretty large surge in suburban sprawl in the 1970s, 1980s, and 1990s, and more apartment construction more recently. Toronto, along with Vancouver, are the only cities that have seen detached homes decline as a percentage of all homes over the past twenty-five years.

## Toronto: Housing Stock

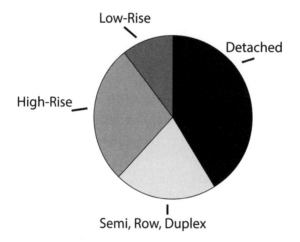

Source: CMHC, 2011.

Not all that surprisingly, housing starts have also ebbed and flowed as demand for housing and housing prices have risen and fallen. The home ownership rate in Toronto is 68 percent, slightly above average compared to all other metropolitan areas across Canada, at 66 percent, but below Canada's overall home ownership rate of 69 percent.

Over the last several decades of Toronto's growth, two additional notable features have affected the development of the city, particularly over the past twenty years: transportation infrastructure and something called the greenbelt.

## TRANSPORTATION

Toronto has seen remarkable population growth. Unfortunately, the city now finds itself the victim of increasing levels of congestion and is frequently cited as having among the worst traffic congestion problems of all cities in North America. The root of this problem is simply a lack of planning and investment in infrastructure.

The city's highways are consistently packed, causing substantial traffic delays on a daily basis — a fact well known by every commuter in the city. The main highways in the area haven't seen any meaningful increase in design capacity since the late 1990s, and in some cases much longer. Over the past twenty-five years, the metropolitan area has seen its population grow by more than 50 percent. But the highways are largely the same.

A lack of expansion of highways on its own doesn't necessarily need to be a problem if a city invests in alternative transportation forms to allow people to get around. Alternative transportation can be subways or commuter trains, streetcars, light rail networks, or other forms of mass transit. Toronto has seen a modest expansion of its subway system, with an underutilized new line running 5.5 kilometres opened in 2002. Another expansion is underway, adding 8.6 kilometres across six new stations, expected to open in 2017.

While the subway system in Toronto is one of the busiest in North America, at just sixty-three kilometres in length and having just sixty-four stations, the system is small relative to the population and geography of the city. Montreal's subway system is slightly larger than Toronto's despite Toronto having a population more than 50 percent larger than Montreal's.

Complementing the subway system, Toronto has 6.4 kilometres of light rail transit across six stations, with another nineteen kilometres across twenty-five stops under construction, and the city also has a significant commuter rail system, with sixty-three stations across 425 kilometres, both expanding the reach of the city's rapid transit.

## GREENBELT

Toronto's rapid growth has outpaced the growth of its transit infrastructure, and this has led to increased commuting times and more congestion. This result has also been a factor in Toronto's trend toward urbanization, which is most visible through the rapid growth of its downtown core population and the boom in condominium construction over the past fifteen years. This boom has continued for a long time and has even accelerated in the years since Toronto's most significant land use policy was introduced, a little over a decade ago.

Toronto's greenbelt was announced in 2004, and the plan was an ambitious one: create one of the largest greenbelts in the world. At over 7,300 square kilometres, or 1.8 million acres, Toronto's greenbelt isn't just large, it's actually larger than the land area of the city it wraps around. Stretching from the shores of Lake Ontario east of Bowmanville; along the edge of Markham up to Lake Simcoe; west to Orangeville, Georgetown, and Milton; then wrapping around Hamilton and St. Catharines, closing the loop on the southwestern shores of Lake Ontario at the U.S. border, the greenbelt prevents zoning-use changes and prevents development within its area. In practical terms, this has made Toronto into an island, significantly limiting the supply of land available for development.

Between the edges of Toronto's suburbs and the inner edges of the greenbelt remains undeveloped land for tens of thousands of new homes, which should provide some supply of single-family and low-rise homes over the next decade or longer. However, tens of thousands of homes is still a small number in relation to the population growth of more than one hundred thousand people each year. It is small also in relation to the millions of homes already existing in the Toronto Census Metropolitan Area.

As the city has grown in size, and particularly since the implementation of the greenbelt around the city, house prices have risen significantly for all types of housing, but particularly for single-family housing.

Toronto: House Prices

Source: CREA.

The nature of land-constrained markets tends to result in higher price-to-income ratios as the limited supply of land increases the cost of housing and wealth-based owners gradually crowd out income-based purchasers.

Similarly, price to rent has risen, particularly over the last decade, following the implementation of the greenbelt.

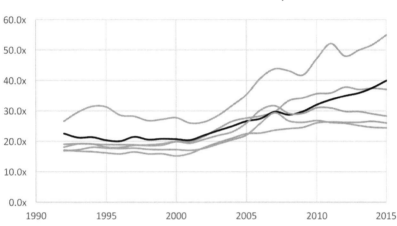

Toronto: Price to Rent Multiples

Note: Toronto is represented by the black line, while the remainder of the six largest cities in Canada are in grey (including Vancouver, the most expensive market).
Source: CMHC, CREA.

This has helped propel average home-price-to-income levels to a range more consistent with other land-constrained markets with healthy population growth, which can often range from five times to as high as twelve times. At 8.5 times currently, Toronto is middle of the pack when it comes to price to income for land-constrained markets but still quite expensive for prospective buyers across all markets.

Looking at the supply of housing in Toronto, the land constraint imposed by the greenbelt suggests most new housing supply for the city will be in the form of high-rise housing over the foreseeable future. The increasing cost of land that results from land constraints, along with continued worsening of congestion in the city, suggests density will continue to increase as developers provide affordable housing supply in the form of condominiums and apartments, where the rising prices of land and higher costs of high-rise construction are overcome by smaller and smaller unit sizes. The high-rise housing developed over the next several years also seems likely to be concentrated in the core of the city, closest to public transit, employment opportunities, and other amenities.

The increasing cost of land resulting from land constraints and worsening congestion suggests density will continue to increase as developers provide affordable housing in the form of condos and apartments.

From a demand perspective, Toronto's broad-based economy, abundance of employment opportunities, and the high appeal its multicultural diversity has in attracting continued strong levels of immigration seem likely to drive continued strong population growth and demand for housing.

Toronto's housing profile seems consistent with a market that has structurally high housing costs and constraints on supply, and is likely to remain expensive, particularly for single-family homes.

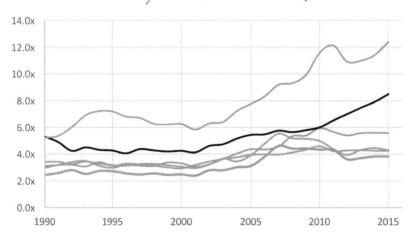

Toronto: Price to Income Multiples

(FIRE stands for Finance, Insurance, and Real Estate.)
Source: CMHC, CREA.

With price to income at an 8.5-times multiple and rising, and price to rent at a 40-times multiple, for the average Torontonian, buying a home for the first time today requires the commitment of a huge proportion of income toward housing costs. This commitment involves elevated risks, including the potential for house prices to decline and interest rates to rise, the latter of which might result in a forced sale, resulting in very expensive transaction costs, or a house-poor lifestyle.

Renting remains a very attractive option, freeing up income for other investments and lifestyle expenses that wouldn't be possible for homeowners. The structure of the Toronto housing market suggests it is likely to remain expensive, even in the event of house price declines, essentially requiring a significantly above-average income and a long time horizon to have buying make sense today.

## MONTREAL

The Montreal CMA is Canada's second-largest city, with a population of 4.1 million. Like Toronto, it has a strong history as one of the most popular destinations for immigrants to Canada. The city's population consists of 23 percent immigrants, including 5 percent considered recent. Despite its appeal as a top immigration destination (the second-most popular destination for most of the past few decades), Montreal's growth rate has been slower than Toronto's but is still a solid 1 percent annually.

The city is ethnically diverse, with a strong francophone demographic and cultural base, 25 percent of Montrealers having French origins. The large "other" component of Montreal's ethnic composition is dominated by those identifying as Canadians.

As is the case in much of the province of Quebec, government employment tends to be higher than the Canadian average, thanks to the province's large government participation in the economy. One of Canada's six largest banks, the smallest, is headquartered in Montreal, with the other five based in Toronto, the largest financial services centre in Canada. Manufacturing and logistics are also relatively large parts of the Montreal economy compared to the Canadian average. Montreal sits in a strategically advantageous spot on the St. Lawrence River and has developed one of the largest inland ports in the world. High volumes of goods transition from ships to rail, and vice versa, in Montreal's port.

## Montreal: Ethnicity

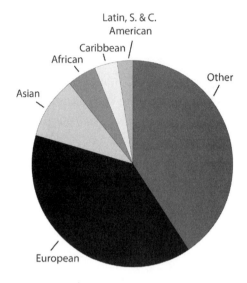

Source: Statistics Canada, 2011.

## Montreal: Employment

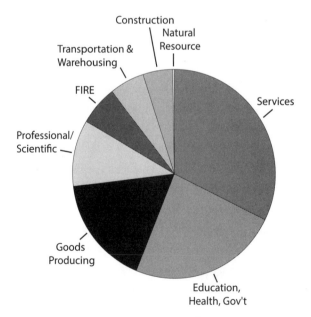

(FIRE stands for Finance, Insurance, and Real Estate.) Source: Statistics Canada, 2011.

The city is a significant education centre, with four large universities, several colleges and other post-secondary educational institutions. Combined, education, healthcare, and government employment account for a large 24 percent of total employment.

Montreal's housing stock is unique among Canadian cities, with a significantly larger proportion of housing in the form of rental units in smaller buildings, like four-plexes, six-plexes, and similar. Montreal has an unusually high proportion of renters, at 45 percent (home ownership is just 55 percent, well below average), compared to the rest of Canada, where 70 percent are homeowners, in part as a result of a greater cultural acceptance of renting.

## Montreal: Housing Stock

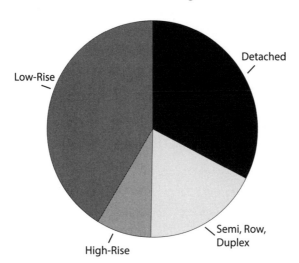

Source: CMHC, 2011.

Montreal has seen a gradual shift toward more and more apartment-style housing over time, after decades of a relatively even split between single-family and apartment-style home construction levels. The style of apartments being built has shifted more recently to include larger buildings with more units, after a relatively short period of building larger buildings in the 1960s and 1970s.

Montreal's subway system is well used, being the busiest system in Canada (by ridership), behind only New York City and Mexico City in North America. With sixty-nine kilometres of track across sixty-eight stations, the system is slightly larger than Toronto's. The last new line added to the Montreal subway was in 1988 (twelve new stations), while an extension adding three new stations was completed in 2007. Despite having a subway system more in keeping with its scale, Montreal is also a congested city. Frequent construction activity on the city's roadways, a lack of expansion of highways, and the natural constraints of bridges and tunnels leave Montrealers complaining frequently about road congestion.

> Montreal has an unusually high proportion of renters, in part as a result of a greater cultural acceptance of renting.

Perhaps the most interesting thing about Montreal when it comes to housing is that it mainly comprises two islands in the St. Lawrence River. More than half of the population of the Census Metropolitan Area lives on these two islands, with the remainder spread around the perimeter on the north and south shores. Being an island, Montreal is a physically land-constrained housing market, putting it into the same category as cities like Manhattan, Hong Kong, Taiwan, and Singapore, where property prices are quite high. The city has a tiny greenbelt of just over forty-nine square kilometres (vs. Toronto's 7,300 square kilometres), which is insignificant compared to the impact of the city's location on two islands.

While there remains undeveloped land on the island of Montreal and more underdeveloped land on the island of Laval, we have already seen the transition toward more high-density housing and expect that trend to continue, which should be supportive of higher prices for housing.

At present, though, house prices in Montreal are relatively low compared to other Canadian cities, both in terms of absolute prices as well as in terms of price to income. At 5.6 times, Montreal's price to income is below the national average of 6.4 times, significantly below Toronto's 8.5 times and less than half of Vancouver's 12.4 times. Each of Montreal, Toronto, and Vancouver has significant land constraints and strong population growth, suggesting above-average prices.

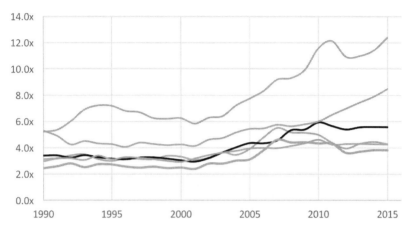

Montreal: Price to Income Multiples

Note: Montreal is represented by the black line, while the remainder of the six largest cities in Canada are in grey (including Vancouver, the most expensive market). Source: CMHC, CREA.

Slightly below-average prices relative to income could reflect a combination of factors, including below-average population growth, a significantly higher share of employment being government-related, the potential for political instability related to sovereignty initiatives, and the language and cultural differences relative to other parts of Canada (potentially reducing inter-provincial migration). It also reflects the skew of the very high price-to-income-levels seen in Vancouver and Toronto and their impact on the average across Canada.

Montreal's price to rent at 37 times is slightly below the Canadian average of 39 times, suggesting house prices might be relatively average in this market. But that conclusion would be wrong.

While price to rent is close to the Canadian average in Montreal, both house prices and rents are below average. It is remarkable how inexpensive renting is in Montreal. At $760 per month, average rents in Montreal are 19 percent below the Canadian average and just a little more than half of the average rent in Vancouver.

Renting in Montreal is clearly a very affordable option, and that might be part of the reason 45 percent of the population are renters.

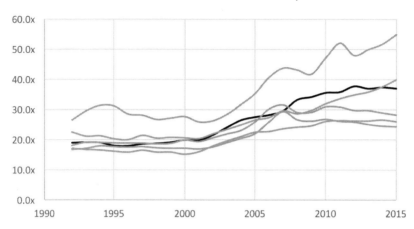

Source: CREA, CMHC.

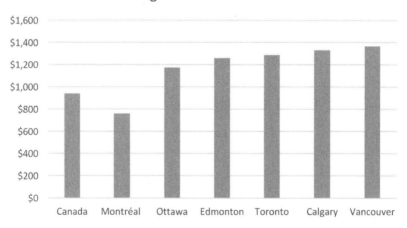

Source: CMHC.

For potential homebuyers, Montreal's housing market also seems pretty reasonably priced, particularly relative to the more expensive markets of Toronto and Vancouver. With significant land constraints and an outlook for continued

TABLE 9.1

| | Population[1] (millions) | Population Growth[1] 15-Year Average | Immigrant Population Share[1] | Price to Income[1 2 3] | Price to Rent[2 3] | Economic Base[1] | Land Constraints | Structural Character |
|---|---|---|---|---|---|---|---|---|
| Toronto | 6.1 | 1.6% | 45.9% | 8.5x | 34.9x | Broadly Diversified | High – Greenbelt Policy | Expensive; Intensifying |
| Montreal | 4.1 | 1.0% | 45.9% | 5.6x | 37.8x | Broadly Diversified, Industrial & Logistics | High – Geographic | Moderate; Slower Growth; Intensifying |
| Vancouver | 2.5 | 1.4% | 40.0% | 12.4x | 48.0x | Diversified, Services Oriented | High – Geographic & Policy | Expensive/Speculative; Intensifying |
| Calgary | 1.4 | 2.8% | 26.2% | 4.3x | 29.8x | Energy Industry & Related | Low | Affordable; Unconstrained; Highly Cyclical |
| Ottawa | 1.3 | 1.3% | 22.6% | 4.2x | 26.2x | Government & Administration | Low | Affordable; Unconstrained; Stable, Low Growth |
| Edmonton | 1.4 | 2.5% | 20.4% | 3.8x | 25.9x | Energy Industry & Related, Government & Education | Low | Affordable; Unconstrained; Cyclical |

1. Statistics Canada
2. CREA
3. CMHC

positive population growth, Montreal looks like quite a low-risk market in which to be a homeowner. Home ownership is well below other markets, sovereignty concerns have faded in recent years, and the market appears to have largely exhausted most of its capacity to supply single-family homes. Montreal's greatest risks from a housing perspective continue to be the potential for political developments to affect population growth and demand for housing.

Across both renting and owning, Montreal is a more affordable market than either Toronto or Vancouver, but it offers the most appealing rental option across all major Canadian markets.

## VANCOUVER

Easily the most expensive major city in Canada for housing, Vancouver is comfortably Canada's third-largest census metropolitan area, with a population of 2.5 million. It is also Canada's third most popular destination for immigrants, occupying a unique position as the closest large North American city to Asia. It shouldn't be surprising that Vancouver's population consists of 40 percent immigrants, including 7 percent considered recent, placing it behind only Toronto in terms of its immigrant share of population. This immigration activity has helped propel Vancouver to an above-average population growth rate of 1.4 percent annually over the past fifteen years (Canada grew at 1 percent).

Demographically, the city's relative proximity to Asia and strong immigration draw is reflected in its ethnicity, with 37 percent of the city of Asian origin. Similar to Montreal, "other" mainly consists of ethnicity reported as Canadian.

The workforce in Vancouver is interesting. The economy tends to be very service-oriented, the result of a large wealthy population relative to the size of the city. In terms of industries, it includes a broad variety of employment, with a strong educational segment, anchored by both University of British Columbia and Simon Fraser University, as well as several smaller universities and colleges; slightly above-average finance, insurance, and real estate employment (FIRE); and exposure to the cyclical paper and forestry industry.

Vancouver is well known for its dense downtown peninsula, where scores of high-rise condos have been built over the past few decades. But, while the city has seen significant high-rise added to its housing stock, Vancouver is still overwhelmingly a low-rise and single-family housing market. High-rise apartments are less than 15 percent of all housing units. Over 60 percent of all homes are individual homes or duplexes.

## Vancouver: Ethnicity

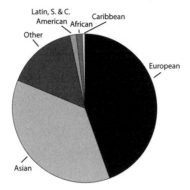

Source: Statistics Canada, 2011.

## Vancouver: Housing Stock

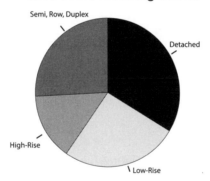

Source: CMHC, 2011.

## Vancouver: Employment

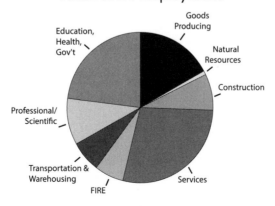

(FIRE stands for Finance, Insurance, and Real Estate.) Source: CMHC, 2011.

Vancouver's rapid population growth and transit strategy have contributed to increasing traffic congestion. Vancouver ranks as the city with the worst congestion of any city in Canada. Strangely enough, its congestion was a choice made by planning officials in the 1970s and 1980s, when they decided against building the multi-lane freeways found in so many other cities. As a result, only the Trans-Canada highway runs through Vancouver, and the city's main arterial roads end up facing more congestion.

These policy decisions seem to have achieved what they purportedly intended to do: create an incentive for more people to use rapid transit, encourage more people to chose to live close to their place of work, and reduce car trips and the related pollution.

Vancouver's public rapid transit system is primarily a three-line rail system spanning sixty-nine kilometres across forty-seven stations called the SkyTrain. The SkyTrain connects at Waterfront Station to the West Coast Express, a single-line rail with eight stops servicing inland to Mission, as well as to the SeaBus and city bus services.

Key to understanding Vancouver's housing market are its physical characteristics. Vancouver is bordered by bodies of water, mountains, and agricultural reserve land. The Fraser River, Burrard Inlet, English Bay, False Creek, and other bodies of water bisect the city. The Agricultural Land Reserve, a provincially administered land reserve spanning 47,000 square kilometres across the province, includes significant lands reserved for agricultural use in Richmond, Delta, Surrey, Langley, and Maple Ridge, as well as in Mission, Abbotsford, and Chilliwack just outside the borders of the Vancouver Census Metropolitan Area. The Agricultural Land Reserve is legislatively a little less restrictive than some greenbelts, but it adds significant land constraints to an already land-constrained market.

Vancouver's land constraints and relatively high population growth rate have led to high house prices. Prices are very high relative to incomes, similar to other significantly land-constrained markets.

Combined with low and declining interest rates, these factors have led to exceptionally high house prices relative to average rents. This very high ratio also reflects the abundance of ground-oriented housing (single-family detached, semi-detached, and duplex), which tends to become expensive

## Vancouver: Price to Income Multiples

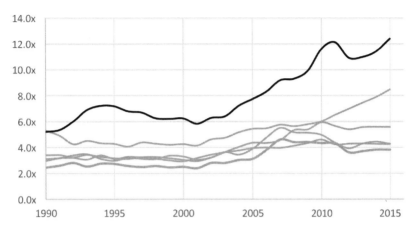

Note: Vancouver is represented by the black line, while the remainder of the six largest cities in Canada are in grey.
Source: CMHC, CREA. Source: CMHC, CREA.

## Vancouver: Price to Rent Multiples

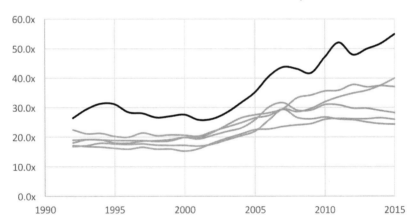

Source: CREA, CMHC.

over time in land-constrained markets. Vancouver in particular has a large number of very expensive homes, including waterfront homes as well as homes with exceptional mountain or ocean views.

While price to rent has consistently been highest in Vancouver, reflecting its long-standing land constraints, at 55 times average rent, the cost of home ownership is extraordinarily high in Vancouver. Its proximity to Asia and Canada's welcoming immigration policies make Vancouver an appealing destination for visitors and investment. It has become more and more apparent that foreign investment has played a key role in the rapid growth in the city's house prices.

Vancouver is uniquely located and offers an attractive climate and natural beauty. However, the foreign investment isn't just a function of the appeal of living in Vancouver, but also of immigration policies, political conditions in China, and other factors not specific to Vancouver. This external influence is dangerous in that changes to political, immigration, or other policies in China and other countries could have a significant impact on Vancouver house prices unrelated to the local economy or housing supply.

When house prices reach such high levels, there is also the risk that pressure builds on politicians to change policies in efforts to reduce the cost of housing. Restrictions on foreign investment, changes to zoning policies to allow new land to be developed (like in the Agricultural Land Reserve, potentially), and changes to taxes, fees, and levies are all possible changes locally that could also affect house prices.

With such elevated house prices, external factors like foreign investment influencing the market, and very low interest rates, owning a home in Vancouver has become much riskier over the past few years. Meanwhile, renting offers a dramatically lower cost of housing and involves none of the risks of ownership. Even if house prices in Vancouver remain stable or rise over the next several years, the cost of owning a home will leave the average Vancouverite house poor and taking a huge bet on house prices.

Vancouver is perhaps the best example of a market in Canada in which renting the Wealthy Renter way is dramatically better than owning a home today.

## CALGARY

They don't call it the wild west for nothing! The city of Calgary's population of 1.4 million has seen Canada's highest population growth rate eleven of the last fifteen years, averaging 2.8 percent annually over that time, well ahead of Toronto at 1.6 percent. While high, Calgary's population growth has varied more, year to year, ranging from 1.7 percent to 3.8 percent, reflecting the boom and bust nature of commodity-driven economies.

The growth of Calgary has resulted in a population base that includes a significant immigrant population (at 26 percent, it's a distant third place to Toronto's 46 percent and Vancouver's 40 percent). Its population is also affected by substantial inter-provincial migration, as a lot of Canadians have been drawn to Calgary for its robust economy and employment opportunities over the past fifteen years. The ethnic make-up of Calgary remains less diverse than other large Canadian cities.

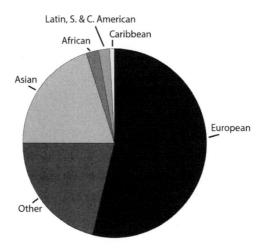

Calgary: Ethnicity

Source: Statistics Canada, 2011.

The driver of this employment and population growth has been high oil and natural gas prices. Calgary is the epicentre of the energy industry in Canada, and high prices have driven huge investments into exploration and development over the past decade, particularly into Alberta's oil sands regions, generating country-leading jobs and wage growth.

## Calgary: Employment

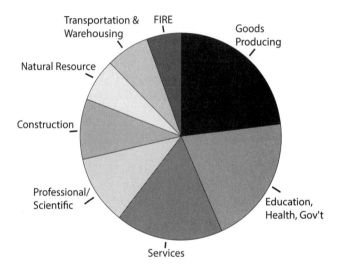

(FIRE stands for Finance, Insurance, and Real Estate.)
Source: Statistics Canada, 2011

Calgary is also one of the youngest cities in Canada, with an average age of thirty-six years compared to the national average of forty-one years as of the last census in 2011. With high-paying jobs and a rapidly growing population, Calgary has seen a dramatic expansion of its housing stock, primarily driven by single-family home construction.

This younger demographic includes a lot of workers starting families, which, combined with high population growth, has led to strong demand for housing.

Since Calgary is situated in the western prairies of Canada, there are no natural limitations to the city's growth outward in any direction for nearly one hundred kilometres, until you pass through the foothills to enter the Rockies.

Calgary: Housing Stock, 1991 | Calgary: Housing Stock, 2011

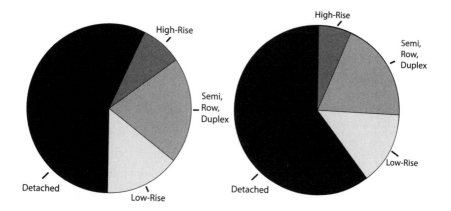

Source: CMHC.

Compared to other large cities, and in particular when compared to Montreal and Toronto, Calgary has very little high-rise housing.

High incomes and relatively low house prices compared to income have helped drive Calgary's home ownership rate to the highest among Canada's big six markets, at around 74 percent.

Like all Canadian cities, Calgary has seen strong house price growth over the past fifteen years, driven to particularly high rates in the early- and mid-2000s by high energy prices and rapid employment, population, and income growth. Despite this rapid growth, price to income in Calgary remains relatively affordable compared to other large Canadian cities, partly due to the city's high average incomes (the highest in Canada), and lack of land constraints.

> High incomes and relatively low house prices compared to income have helped drive Calgary's home ownership rate to the highest among Canada's big six markets.

In 2013 and 2014, the mayor of Calgary and the city planning department began an unofficial shift in planning to try to encourage more high-rise residential construction and less suburban sprawl. The push for more density included a more onerous approvals process for zoning and permitting for single-family homes.

The result was a slowdown in new housing starts as planners tried to curb one of Canada's most sprawling cities. The rapid growth of Alberta and strength of its housing market took a pause in 2015, following a sharp decline in energy prices in the second half of 2014, and began to see erosion in 2016, as low energy prices persisted. The efforts of the planning department and mayor proved fortuitous, helping prevent a more significant decline in housing conditions in Calgary in 2014, 2015, and 2016 as energy prices fell. The city's planning policies could have a significant impact on the type of housing built in the future to accommodate growth if the price of oil rebounds, the economy recovers, and the city returns to rapid population growth. With one of the highest proportions of detached housing of any major Canadian city, significantly higher than all but Edmonton, Calgary's housing market could see significant policy changes.

With the heavy exposure of its employment and capital investment to energy market conditions, combined with no natural constraints on the growth of the city, Calgary's housing market is structurally set up to be among the most volatile and difficult to forecast of Canada's large cities. That means high population and employment growth when energy prices are high and rising, and flat or even potentially declining population when energy prices fall for sustained periods. Calgary house prices rose an astounding 39 percent in 2006, only to fall 7 percent in 2008 and 2009. In 2015, Calgary house prices fell 1.7 percent, with further declines expected in 2016, following the sharp decline in employment that accompanied the declines in energy prices in 2014 and 2015.

The volatility in income, population, and house prices, along with no structural constraints on land, have created a lot of fluctuations in housing market metrics but still a relatively affordable housing market compared to other Canadian cities.

Along with Ottawa and Edmonton, Calgary remains quite reasonably priced, at close to 4 times price to income. From a renter's perspective, house prices are high, but not as high relative to rent as prices in Vancouver and Toronto. At 28 times price to rent, renting a home remains quite attractive in Calgary, not only because the cost is quite low, but also because of the volatility created by the city's high dependence on energy industry employment and investment.

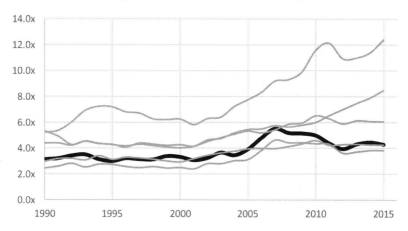

## Calgary: Price to Income Multiples

Note: Calgary is represented by the black line, while the remainder of the six largest cities in Canada are in grey (including Vancouver, the most expensive market).
Source: CMHC, CREA.

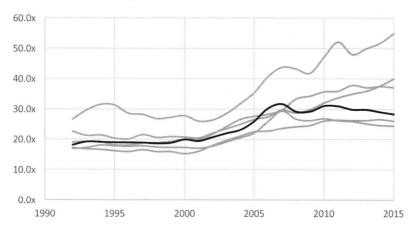

## Calgary: Price to Rent Multiples

Source: CREA, CMHC.

The significant employment and economic reliance of Calgary on the energy industry, and the resulting volatility in demand for housing, can result in significant swings in house prices, which has been evident over much of the past decade.

## Calgary: Home Prices

Source: CREA.

While the relatively affordable pricing of homes in Calgary might suggest it is a market where home ownership makes more sense, the less-diversified economy, reliance on the cyclical energy industry, and lack of land constraints tend to make Calgary's housing market more volatile. With home ownership often forming the core of homeowner savings, volatility in house prices, and particularly volatility in employment in the city, pose significant risks to homeowners.

Renting in Calgary provides flexibility to adapt to changing economic conditions, which can be particularly important for workers in the energy or related industries. In the wake of the recent declines in energy sector investment and employment, and with house prices remaining largely unchanged, renting is clearly the more favourable option in Calgary today.

## OTTAWA

The nation's capital region is a relative bastion of stability. While the Ottawa CMA doesn't have any significant constraints on growth, this city of 1.3 million people tends to see very consistent but gradual population — averaging 1.3 percent per year — and employment growth.

From an immigration perspective, Ottawa is a laggard, ranking seventh as a destination behind Winnipeg, Canada's seventh largest city, despite the nation's capital being more than 65 percent larger than Manitoba's capital city. Lacking the strong draw for immigrants, but also being the capital of Canada, Ottawa has an immigrant share of population of 22.6 percent. The resulting ethnic diversity is significantly less than that of Toronto, Montreal, or Vancouver, Canada's top destinations for immigrants.

## Ottawa: Ethnicity

Source: Statistics Canada, 2011.

The stability of the city is rooted in its high share of employment by the federal government, which accounts for more than 20 percent of all jobs in the CMA. The city also has significant healthcare and education employment, which, along with government, account for over 40 percent of all Ottawa employment compared to Canada's other large cities, where education, healthcare, and government employment account for 20 to 24 percent of all employment.

The city has four large hospitals, including Queensway-Carlton, Ottawa, Montfort, and the Children's Hospital of Eastern Ontario, as well as a number of smaller specialty hospitals. Ottawa is also home to University of Ottawa and Carleton University, as well as Algonquin College and La Cité collégiale.

## Ottawa: Employment

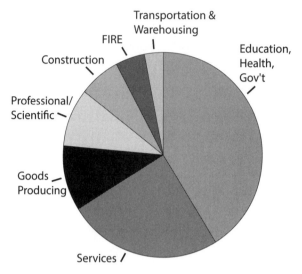

(FIRE stands for Finance, Insurance, and Real Estate.) Source: Statistics Canada, 2011.

Government, healthcare, and educational employment tend to have little cyclicality and be relatively immune to economic conditions.

Similar to Calgary, the housing stock is mostly ground-oriented housing (detached, semi-detached, row, or duplex), comprising 72 percent of all homes and reflecting a relative lack of land constraints, with a notably low share of low-rise housing.

## Ottawa: Housing Stock

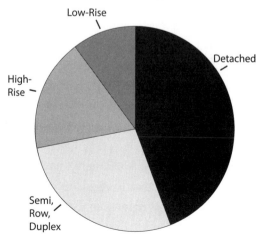

Source: CMHC, 2011.

Ottawa's low-density housing makes it more similar to Calgary and Edmonton than Montreal, Vancouver, and Toronto.

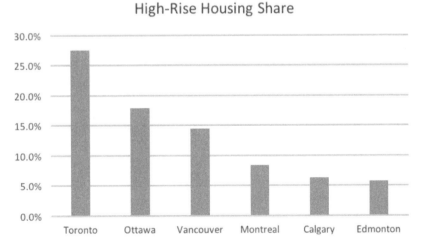

As with Toronto, Ottawa's growth has included periods of significant growth in housing stock concentrated on high-rise buildings. So while Ottawa is mainly ground-oriented housing, where the city has higher-density housing, it's mainly high-rise. In fact, Ottawa has more high-rise housing than Vancouver.

**Source: CMHC.**

Ottawa's transportation infrastructure is heavily car-oriented, with rapid transit consisting of a one-line light rail system extending eight kilometres across five stations, with a second line under construction adding 12.5 kilometres across thirteen stations. The first line was completed in 2001, while the second is expected to be completed in 2017 or 2018. Further expansion has been proposed, but is not yet underway. The light rail is complemented by a bus transit system, including express lines with dedicated lanes.

The relatively small existing rapid transit line, combined with development of an expanded system, has the potential to affect property values, and probably already has for homes close to future stations under construction.

The city, including Gatineau, straddles the Ontario–Quebec border and the Ottawa River and has no significant constraints on growth. Ottawa has a greenbelt, although it is less than 3 percent of the size of the greenbelt that surrounds Toronto, and the city has already substantially expanded beyond the inner and outer boundaries of the designated areas.

Not surprisingly, the city's highly stable employment profile and lack of significant land constraints have resulted in Ottawa remaining one of the more affordable housing markets in the country, with average price to income a reasonable 4.2 times.

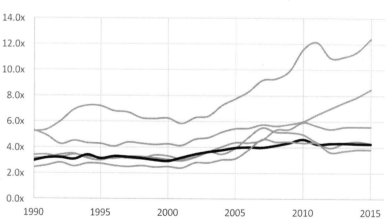

**Ottawa: Price to Income Multiples**

Note: Ottawa is represented by the black line, while the remainder of the six largest cities in Canada are in grey (including Vancouver, the most expensive market).
Source: CREA, Statistics Canada.

The balanced supply and demand conditions in Ottawa, as well as the stability of employment and economic activity, also extend to the rental market, where price to rent remains among the lowest of major Canadian cities at 26 times. This level is high relative to historical levels, similar to all Canadian markets, but doesn't suggest extreme levels of house price risk.

## Ottawa: Price to Rent Multiples

Source: CREA, CMHC.

The high degree of stability of economic and population growth in Ottawa, as well as the high degree of stability provided by the abundance of federal government jobs, has led to a healthy balance between the supply and demand of housing, reaching a price-to-income equilibrium that reflects stability and confidence (pushing up on prices) and adequate supply (tending to constrain prices). With stability and consistent growth, Ottawa should see relative stability in house prices, compared to other Canadian centres.

While I make the case repeatedly throughout this book that renting can be a better option than buying a home, in Ottawa home ownership offers a reasonable option for homeowners with the

Stable economic and population growth, as well as stable government jobs, has led to a healthy balance between the supply and demand of housing.

stability of government employment at relatively affordable prices. With the right savings discipline, renting should provide better returns than Ottawa homes, but at least the risks of home ownership are lower in Ottawa.


## EDMONTON

Canada's sixth largest city has a population of 1.2 million, making it the second largest in Alberta, after Calgary. Edmonton has a unique blend of Calgary's high growth, but cyclical economy, and Ottawa's government-driven stability. Population growth has been strong over the past fifteen years, averaging 2.5 percent, second to Cagary's 2.8 percent average, reflecting mainly growth in energy sector employment, with its proximity to the province's oil sands regions.

The abundance of employment growth has propelled Edmonton into the fifth most popular destination for immigrants, up from eighth in 2001, more than tripling the number of annual arrivals. Despite the increased level of immigration in recent years, the city remains less diverse than most other large Canadian cities, with three-quarters identifying ethnicity as European or Canadian.

### Edmonton: Ethnicity

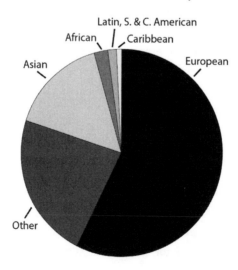

Source: Statistics Canada, 2011.

The economy of Edmonton is a barbell of stability and growth. Because it's the capital city of Alberta, a significant portion of employment is government-related, augmented by healthcare and educational employment, while the energy industry has been the driver of growth.

Edmonton is home to four large hospitals, as well as a number of smaller hospitals, clinics, and research institutes. It's also home to the University of Alberta, MacEwan University, and a number of colleges and other post-secondary institutions.

While Calgary is the head office capital of the Alberta energy industry, Edmonton is the closest major city to Alberta's Athabasca, Cold Lake, and Peace River oil sands deposits. It serves as a regional hub for much of the people and goods going to and from Fort McMurray, Grande Prairie, and Lloydminster. This is reflected in the city's high (14 percent) employment in the construction industry, well ahead of second-place Calgary at 9 percent, Vancouver at 8 percent, and the other three ranging from 5 to 7 percent. Direct resource-related employment in Edmonton accounts for half as much of total employment as it does in Calgary, but is still more than five times higher a share of employment than in Vancouver (which is more mining and forestry) and 15 times or more higher than Toronto, Ottawa, and Montreal. This exposure creates significant energy-industry-driven cyclicality in Edmonton's growth. The city also has the lowest level of finance, insurance, and real estate employment among Canada's big six markets, slightly lower than second-place Ottawa.

Like the unconstrained cities of Calgary and Ottawa, Edmonton has accommodated its rapid population growth with mainly ground-oriented housing, which accounts for 76 percent of all homes.

Edmonton's rapid transit is a two-line light rail system with eighteen stations spanning twenty-four kilometres. The Capital Line runs from south central Edmonton north through downtown, then turns northeast. It was first opened in 1978, with five stations spanning six kilometres, and was expanded by four stations in the 1980s, one in the 1990s, and another five since 2006. The Metro Line opened in 2015, adding 3.3 kilometres across three new stations, and overlaps with seven stations on the Capital Line.

With little in the way of constraints on land availability, house prices in Edmonton have seen significant growth along with the city's population growth and high average incomes (although, as with Calgary, the recent decline in energy-industry investment and employment has brought

## Edmonton: Employment

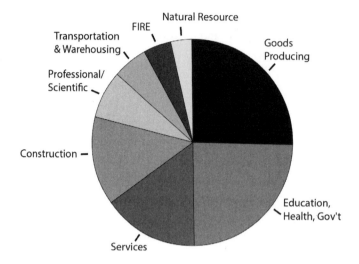

(FIRE stands for Finance, Insurance, and Real Estate.)
Source: Statistics Canada, 2011.

## Edmonton: Housing Stock

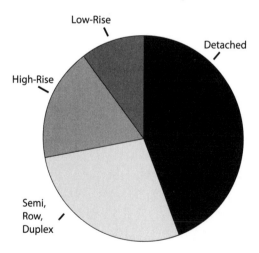

Source: CMHC, 2011.

this growth to a halt). Even when the economy was booming, however, house prices were less expensive than in most major cities in Canada on a price-to-income basis.

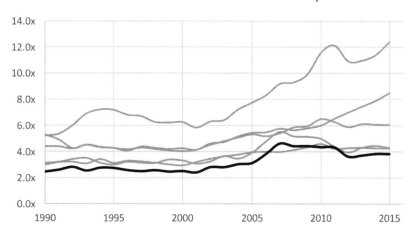

Note: Edmonton is represented by the black line, while the remainder of the six largest cities in Canada are in grey (including Vancouver, the most expensive market). Source: CMHC, CREA.

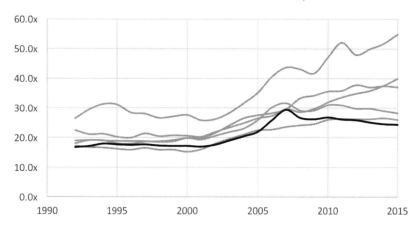

Source: CREA, CMHC.

Like many cities, Edmonton has set priorities of increasing density, with a goal of 25 percent of new residential units being created in mature neighbourhoods. There are no physical land constraints and no policy constraints currently in place. The city continues to see substantial low-density construction but has seen an uptick in high-rise and apartment-style housing starts over the past few years. Combined with a lack of significant land constraints, the city has seen price to rent remain relatively stable, currently 24 times, significantly lower than the Canadian average of 39 times and less than half the multiple in Vancouver.

The lack of significant land constraints in Edmonton suggest house prices are unlikely to rise much beyond five times average income, while the recent weakness in the prices of oil and gas and the related slowdown in investment could result in declining average incomes. While Edmonton has the attractive and stabilizing feature of significant government employment, it remains exposed to energy industry cycles, making its housing market more prone to sharp price increases and decreases. Similar to Calgary, home ownership in Edmonton exposes homeowners to the volatility of the energy sector, offsetting the benefits of relatively less expensive housing, while the lack of land constraints limits long-term price appreciation with plenty of capacity for new housing.

> Home ownership in Edmonton exposes homeowners to the volatility of the energy sector, offsetting the benefits of relatively less expensive housing.

Edmonton's housing market should continue to remain among the more affordable of major Canadian markets. Population and economic growth, and in particular growth of energy-industry investment, will continue to have a large impact on housing prices in Edmonton.

⊚   ⊚   ⊚

Across Canada's six largest cities, where nearly half of Canadians live and where most of our population growth is occurring, conditions vary significantly. Falling interest rates and rising home ownership have contributed to strong house price appreciation across all six markets over the past fifteen years.

In Toronto, Montreal, and Vancouver, broadly diversified economies, high population growth rates, and significant land constraints form ideal conditions for consistently expensive housing markets. Both Vancouver and Toronto have seen detached homes fall as a percentage of total housing, as land constraints and higher prices have driven growth in high-density housing construction. Montreal house prices remain more affordable than Vancouver and Toronto prices, reflecting slightly slower population growth and continued supply of detached homes. However, there is limited remaining undeveloped land, and density is rising, making Montreal the safest of the three cities in which to own a home. Across all three of these cities, renting offers substantially less risk, as well as a much less expensive way to live.

Calgary, Edmonton, and Ottawa have very few constraints on growth, which puts a limit on how much more expensive housing in these markets can get. Demand in these markets is met with supply, and primarily in the form of detached homes. Energy prices and energy industry investment and employment are dominant factors in demand for housing in Calgary and, to a slightly lesser extent, Edmonton. Ottawa's relatively affordable housing market, with its steady employment and average growth rate, should provide consistent, stable, and relatively affordable house prices.

Among the six cities, Vancouver and Toronto offer the greatest cost savings to renters, with home ownership exceptionally expensive and house prices at extremely high levels. Calgary and Edmonton are more affordable but expose homeowners to the cyclical risk of energy-industry investment and employment, making renting a cheaper and lower-risk option.

Montreal and Ottawa offer the least risky home ownership options across these markets, with relative stable markets, diversified employment, steady population growth, and house prices that are high by historical standards but relatively affordable compared to Vancouver and Toronto. Despite these lower risk profiles, in both Ottawa and Montreal renting is significantly cheaper than home ownership.

That doesn't sound so bad, does it? House prices have been rising for a long time, and very clearly housing has made a lot of people a lot of money, right?

Let's look at the ugly numbers to find out.

# CHAPTER 10
## The Ugly Numbers

Home ownership in Canada has a great reputation as a successful investment strategy. Popular opinion is that housing has beaten most other investments and has done so with lower risk and volatility than other common investments, like stocks or bonds.

There are a lot of reasons for this strong reputation, like the fact that houses have gone up over time in Canada, particularly recently; because houses are many Canadians' largest and only significant store of wealth, accounting for 38 percent of total household assets (StatCan); and because the math around calculating investment returns isn't well understood. Everyone knows someone who bought a house for one price and years later sold it for a whole lot more. That also helps housing's reputation as a strong investment.

Before we get to the numbers, we need to have a brief chat about how we define investment returns. Investment returns are a little more complicated than just sale price minus purchase price.

If you bought a stock at $100 dollars and sold it later at $150, you made $50 on an investment of $100. In percentage terms, that works out to a 50-percent return.

Seems like a pretty good return. But is it?

What else do we need to know to tell if it was a good return?

If it took six months, then that is completely different than if it took a full year. If the goal of investing is to achieve the highest returns, the faster the investment delivers that positive return, the better. For this reason, the investment industry tends to compare investments based on an annual rate of return.

If our $100 investment is sold at $150 after one year, it has provided a 50-percent annual return. If it was sold at $150 after six months, then the annualized rate of return would be much higher.

If you invest $100 and receive $150 after six months, then re-invest the $150 into another investment that then rises 50 percent over the next six months, the end result would be $100 × 1.5 × 1.5 = $225. So the return is $225 – $100 = a $125 profit from a $100 investment, which equals a 125-percent annual return. That's two and a half times the return over the one-year period, compared to the 50 percent return. If, instead, it took six years to get to $150, then the investment return would be a much lower 7 percent per year.

We need to know how long it took for the stock to go from $100 to $150. Clearly, the time frame over which the return is generated is a pretty important factor.

Another important factor is whether there were any other payments made during the investment period. These payments could include dividend payments received or other payments made into the investment. In our $100 investment scenario, if the investment was sold after a year at $150, but there was also a $30 dividend paid during the year, the investment return is significantly different. This time the return would be $150 + $30 = $180 of ending value. That divided by the starting value of $100 provides an 80-percent return.

If, however, instead of a dividend, there was a $20 commission paid when you bought the shares and another $20 commission paid when you sold them, your return looks a lot different: $150 – $20 = $130 of ending value, divided by the starting value, or cost, of $100 + $20 = $120, providing an 8.3-percent return.

The important thing to remember here is that the investment return is the total amount you are left with, after all revenues and expenses, compared to what you "invested" to begin with, including transaction costs. It's too easy to forget about transaction costs and costs that can be incurred in between the purchase and sale, so we need to pay close attention to all of the costs.

Another thing we need in order to determine if an investment provided a good return is something to compare it to.

If I bought a stock that went from $100 to $150 over the course of a year, providing a 50-percent return, I might think that's a pretty good return. But if you told me you bought a different stock and it went from $100 to $200 during that same year, providing a 100-percent return, my 50-percent return doesn't look as good.

To compare investment returns accurately, we need to know: 1) the total investment (purchase price plus other costs); 2) the total proceeds (ending price plus any income, minus any other expenses related to the investment); 3) the time frame over which the investment took place; and 4) some other investment performances to compare the investment return against.

Now that we have a basic set of rules that we'll use to compare housing to other investments, let's look at some history.

The reputation of housing as an investment is one that tends to swing with the winds of local house prices. Recent house price performance is obviously an important factor in housing investment returns. However, too often that calculation is quite closely tied to recent price performance, with much less focus on long-term performance.

It is true that Canadian house prices, and those in many other countries, have generally increased over long periods of time.

Average Canadian Home Price

Source: CREA.

That makes a lot of sense to me. After all, a house is made up of materials, like wood, concrete, copper pipes, steel, and bricks. To put those materials together to make a house requires labour, and both materials and labour tend to go up in price over time. So, the cost to build a house goes up over time. This fact, combined with any amount of population growth, means that as new houses are required, the cost of building new houses will rise as well.

But has the house price appreciation shown above delivered good investment returns?

The first thing we can look at is the price appreciation of Canadian homes compared to the S&P/TSX Composite Index, which is the broadest group of Canadian companies you can purchase through a single investment on the Toronto Stock Exchange (via low-cost Exchange Traded Funds, most simply). There are about 235 companies included in the index: Canadian banks, railway companies, energy companies, pipelines and utilities, cable and telecommunications companies, mining companies, grocers, technology companies, real estate trusts and companies, and healthcare companies.

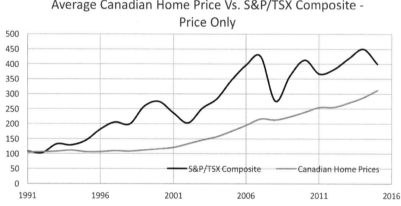

Average Canadian Home Price Vs. S&P/TSX Composite - Price Only

Source: CREA, Bloomberg.

Based on the graph above, it looks like houses in Canada have been okay investments, with prices rising at a compound annual return of 4.7 percent over the twenty-five years to December 31, 2015. Meanwhile, the S&P/TSX Composite Index has seen its price rise at a compound annual return of 5.7 percent over the same period. That may not sound like a big difference, but when you look at how much $100 invested in each would be after twenty-five years, it's a bigger deal. An investment of $100 in Canadian house prices twenty-five years ago would be worth about $312 today, while the same $100 invested in the S&P/TSX Composite Index would be worth $399 today, or about 28 percent more.

So there was a better return from stocks than there was from housing over that twenty-five-year period. But you could make the argument that house prices were more steady and reliable, with less volatility. That may be true, but the above analysis isn't complete.

As we discussed previously, price isn't the only factor in returns. We need to consider the other revenues and expenses that go along with the investments. The S&P/TSX Composite Index, and most other indexes, provide dividend income on a regular basis. If we include the dividend income from the S&P/TSX Composite Index, the returns look a little less compelling for housing.

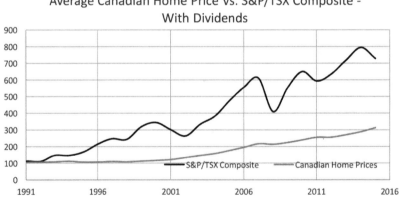

Average Canadian Home Price Vs. S&P/TSX Composite - With Dividends

Source: CREA, Bloomberg.

When you include the dividend income of the index, the return gap between the two widens, with the S&P/TSX Composite Index delivering an 8.2-percent annual return over twenty-five years, while house prices are still 4.7 percent. A wider gap, but the magnitude of the difference is even more stark when you consider that $100 in the index for twenty-five years grows to become $728, while $100 still grows to $318. That's a much larger, 129-percent higher return from stocks than from housing over the twenty-five-year period, leaving you with more than twice as much at the end.

But we're not done yet. Houses have what is basically a negative dividend in the form of maintenance costs, property taxes, and utility costs. This is where it gets a little bit messy. Homes are neither 100-percent accommodation nor 100-percent investment. They're a blend of the two, and there isn't a clear line where it changes from one to the other.

A renter has to pay rent to their landlord. The beauty of rent is that you know exactly what you're getting for your rent payments: the right to occupy the house for a specific period of time. Typically, there will be a lease that outlines who is responsible for which payments, like the electricity, water, and heat. In most cases, property taxes are paid by the landlord out of the rent.

Everybody has to live somewhere. By that line of thinking, a certain portion of the cost of living in a house would need to be paid whether a person owned a home or rented one. So when we're trying to compare the investment performance of a house to a stock market index, it would be unfair to deduct all of these

> As investments, houses have what is basically a negative dividend in the form of maintenance costs, property taxes, and utility costs.

expenses. However, homeowners are more likely to spend a little more than a landlord would on maintenance items, and they also fail to account for the time they spend maintaining their home. Each homeowner will have a different approach, but I'll conservatively estimate that 1 percent per year is what homeowners pay in maintenance and other costs above what a landlord might choose to spend, which should also account for the time homeowners spend performing maintenance tasks they wouldn't otherwise do if they were renting.

The investment returns of housing are starting to look less attractive as we start to include the ongoing costs.

Including an assumed 1 percent ongoing annual cost of ownership, the house price returns of home ownership have driven the $100 invested in a house in 1991 from $318, before ongoing costs, to just $271 — significantly less than the $728 the S&P/TSX Composite Index delivered, including dividends. That leaves homeowner returns down to 4.1 percent annually, compared to the stock index more than twice as high, at 8.3 percent. Now the return differential is getting so wide it can't be ignored.

We're still missing some important costs. Ones that relate explicitly to an owned home that don't exist for rented homes.

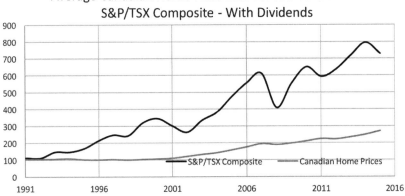

Average Canadian Home Price Less 1% Annual Cost Vs. S&P/TSX Composite - With Dividends

Source: CREA, Bloomberg.

These are indisputable items: 1) brokerage fees; 2) land transfer taxes; 3) mortgage insurance; and 4) title insurance, survey costs, legal expenses, and other costs. Brokerage fees in Canada and the United States average 5 percent and are paid by the seller. Land transfer taxes exist in many provinces and cities, including British Columbia, Manitoba, Ontario, and Quebec, among others. They can reach more than 3.5 percent of the purchase price and are payable by the buyer of the property. Mortgage insurance is required for all Canadian mortgages obtained from federally regulated lenders in which the buyer makes a down payment of less than 20 percent. The fee is variable, rising to 3.35 percent for mortgages with only 5-percent down payments. The title insurance, survey costs, and legal fees are individually relatively small but can add up to as much as 2 percent or more of the purchase price.

All together, transaction costs can easily exceed 5 percent of the purchase price when buying and 5 percent of the sale price when selling.

Let's have another look at that last chart, but this time we'll make the following adjustments:

- Each house price is increased by 5 percent at the start of the period, and reduced by 5 percent at the end of the period, reflecting the transactions costs associated with buying and selling homes.
- Each house price is also reduced by 1 percent at the end of each year, to reflect the cost of homeowner maintenance, property taxes, and other homeowner expenses not incurred by renters.
- For the S&P/TSX Composite, we have added a 0.5-percent commission to the initial cost of the investment and deducted the same cost at the end of the period, to reflect the much lower but still material transaction costs associated with buying an exchange-traded index fund.
- For the S&P/TSX Composite, we have deducted 0.2 percent at the end of each year, to reflect the management cost of a passive index ETF investment.

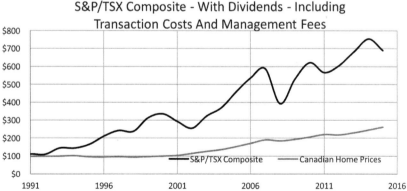

Average Canadian Home Price Less 1% Annual Cost Vs. S&P/TSX Composite - With Dividends - Including Transaction Costs And Management Fees

Source: CREA, Bloomberg.

Once you add those costs into the comparison, you can see that housing hasn't done all that well. After all of the costs, the return on the S&P/TSX Composite Index drops from 8.3 percent to 8 percent on a compounded annual return basis, growing $100 invested at the end of 1990 to $689 at the end of 2015 after paying commission on the sale. By comparison, the return on Canadian house prices has now dropped to 3.7 percent on a compound annual basis, down from an original 4.6 percent, before we had considered transaction costs and ongoing costs. That $100 invested into housing at the end of 1990 turns out to have grown to only $261 after considering all of the associated costs. That means that investing in stocks delivered more than two and a half times as much money to investors than housing did over the past twenty-five years. Two and a half times!

Very clearly, Canadian house prices haven't delivered returns anywhere near those of the Canadian stock market, particularly when you consider the additional amounts of money invested into houses, like kitchen and bathroom renovations, that are not captured by house price indexes and come on top of the normal maintenance costs we deducted earlier.

If you really want to make the comparison look worse, consider what investment returns would be if house prices actually went down, like they did a decade ago in the United States.

## ACE IN THE HOLE?

Before we move on, there are a couple of additional things to cover when comparing investment returns of homes to stocks. Many people think about the first of these things as the "ace in the hole" for Canadian housing, the thing that really makes it a great investment. That is the principal residence exception to capital gains in Canada.

Canadian house prices haven't delivered returns anywhere near those of the Canadian stock market.

Normally, when a Canadian buys an investment at one price and sells it later at a higher price, they have to pay tax on the difference, known as capital gains. It is true that there is no tax payable on the increase in the value of a primary residence, and that is indeed an attractive feature of owning a home in Canada. In fact, it's one of the housing policy tools that the government uses to encourage home owner-ship. More on that later.

But the importance of this tax exemption is often overstated — for a few reasons. The first is that tax rates vary, depending on a person's income in a given year. The tax rate on capital gains is half of the tax rate on ordinary income, which translates to a rate of about 15 percent for the average indi-vidual Canadian, rising to as much as 27 percent for top earners in the highest tax province (Nova Scotia). Assuming the worst-case scenario — being a Nova Scotian earning more than $200,000 per year — the com-pound annual return on the S&P/TSX Composite Index, after paying capital gains on a sale after twenty-five years, is reduced from 8 percent to 6.9 percent. This still dramatically outperforms house prices at 3.9 percent, after considering all of the costs of home ownership.

In reality, homeowners often buy and sell homes more than once every twenty-five years, which can also be the case for investors in stocks. The prin-cipal residence exemption becomes more significant, from a tax perspective, as a homeowner buys and sells more homes, resulting in the potential for multiple capital gains that would otherwise be taxable.

However, any potential benefit from avoiding capital gains on such home sales is more than offset by the other transaction costs that are incurred each time a home is sold, including land transfer taxes, brokerage fees, legal fees, and other costs. These costs typically amount to 5 percent or more of the value of a home for each purchase and each sale. That means that each time a homeowner moves, they are paying 10 percent of the value of their home in transaction costs.

Given the dramatic negative impact on returns I demonstrated when a 5-percent transaction cost was added at the beginning and again at the end of the twenty-five-year period, as well as an annual 1-per-cent "maintenance and other" cost, it's safe to say that the more times a homeowner moves, the worse their investment return becomes.

Another thing we should cover here is the volatility of stock prices.

> Given the dramatic negative impact transaction costs and additional maintenance have on returns, it's safe to say that the more times a homeowner moves, the worse their investment return becomes.

This is one of the most commonly cited reasons for not investing in the stock market. The ups and downs of stock markets make a lot of people uncomfortable. Volatility is often confused with risk, and, as a result, many people believe stocks are more risky than homes as investments. There is no denying that stock prices move up and down with a lot more frequency and transparency than home values. It is the frequency with which stock prices move up and down that makes people remember volatility.

It's easy to understand how one might look at Canadian house prices and assume they only ever go up — it's been more than twenty years since there was a significant and sustained downturn. In fact, the last major crash in Canadian house prices happened in the late 1980s and early 1990s. Even for those Canadians who were homeowners more than twenty-five years ago, the memories, emotions, and thought processes that accompany a housing crash have long since been replaced by year after year of house price gains. That is exactly the time when the risk of an overheated housing market rises — when it's been so long since house prices dropped sharply that people have nearly forgotten that house prices can fall.

When house prices do fall, the casualties are high. Just ask any American who bought a home in 2006. Homes are typically bought with leverage and the cycles are long, meaning that if house prices go down, they can go down and stay down for years, and in some cases indefinitely. And, of course, homes are typically a homeowner's largest asset.

The past twenty-five years, which is the time frame I analyzed in this chapter, is interesting specifically because it has been such an incredible period for Canadian house prices. Interest rates have fallen nearly ten percentage points, the Canadian home ownership rate has risen from 62.6 percent in 1991 to more than 69 percent today, and Canada's population has grown almost 29 percent. Despite these favourable conditions, homes have significantly underperformed Canada's largest stocks. Ugly numbers indeed!

So why does home ownership have such a reputation for creating wealth?

# CHAPTER 11
## Leverage: Seductive and Deadly

We've looked at historical price growth for houses and found it's not all that impressive once you include all the costs. In fact, it's pretty disappointing if you think about how the returns compare to the reputation housing has for making people rich. That's because the returns are only part of the story. The real answer to why housing has such a great reputation is leverage.

Unlike renters, who pay their rent in full each month, people who buy houses only pay a small portion of the purchase price, known as a down payment, when they buy a house. The rest is borrowed from a bank, credit union, or other lender. The borrowed portion, called a mortgage, is a commitment to pay the remainder of the purchase price over a long period of time, or when you sell the house. The down payment is what initially makes up the equity in the purchase of a house (equity + mortgage = purchase price).

The reason most people do this is because houses are very expensive. The average Canadian house costs just over $500,000, according to the Canadian Real Estate Association (CREA). That means the average house in Canada costs more than seven times the average household income of Canadians — before income tax! House prices are now over nine times the average after-tax income of a Canadian household. After considering all of the other things after-tax income is spent on (like food, clothing, and transportation), it's easy to see how, for many Canadians, homes now cost more than a lifetime of savings.

And so, when people buy houses, they use only a small amount of their own money, and a lot of borrowed money, to buy a very expensive possession. This is known as leverage, and its impact on investment returns can be profound. Effectively, a small down payment is "leveraged" to provide the returns generated by the much larger asset. Let's take a look at a couple of examples to make it a bit clearer.

Jen wants to buy a house, and she's saved up $30,000 over the last five years to serve as a down payment. She goes to the bank, and they agree to lend her a mortgage of $270,000. Together with her down payment, the mortgage allows Jen to buy a $300,000 house.

So Jen finds a house she likes that costs $300,000 and buys it.

In investment terms, Jen has invested $30,000 with 10 times leverage ($300,000 ÷ $30,000) to buy a $300,000 asset.

Now Jen's investment of $30,000 is exposed to the change in price of the total asset (the $300,000 house), which means the change in value of her down payment will be 10 times the change in value of the total asset. That is, if the price of the house goes up 1 percent, her equity value would increase by 10 percent (10 × 1 percent = 10 percent).

Jen's house was worth $300,000 when she bought it. Then it went up 1 percent. That means the house is now worth $303,000 ($300,000 × 101 percent).

Now, because Jen borrowed $270,000 of the purchase price, she still owes $270,000 on her mortgage, but when the house price goes up, the mortgage remains the same. So now Jen's equity (from her $30,000 down payment) is worth $33,000 ($303,000 – $270,000). And that is 10 percent more than what her down payment was, resulting in a 10 percent return.

I already touched on transaction costs in the last chapter and how significantly they can affect returns. So we know that, in reality, there are costs associated with selling a house that would reduce this return significantly. However, to make it easier to demonstrate the effects of leverage, we've ignored them for the above example.

Now imagine Jen's house has gone up 10 percent. In recent history there are lots and lots of examples of housing markets where prices have risen 10 percent or more over the course of even just a few years. There are even markets where prices have risen much more than 10 percent in a single year.

If Jen's house were to go up 10 percent, her investment return on her $30,000 down payment would be an amazing 100 percent. That is, her house would be worth $330,000 ($300,000 × 110 percent) and, with her mortgage of $270,000 taken out, Jen's equity would be worth $60,000 ($330,000 – $270,000), or twice the down payment she'd initially invested.

The amount of leverage depends on the amount of the down payment compared to the purchase price. As the amount a person invests as their down payment decreases compared to the total cost of the house, the amount of leverage increases.

A $30,000 down payment on a $300,000 house (10 percent down payment) generates 10 times leverage ($300,000 ÷ $30,000). A $60,000 down payment (20 percent) on a $300,000 house is 5 times leverage ($300,000 ÷ $60,000). A $6,000 down payment (2 percent) would be 50 times ($300,000 ÷ $6,000).

The higher the leverage, the more the change in house price is magnified or "levered" for the return on the investment of the down payment. At 5 times leverage, a 10 percent change in house price would generate a 50-percent return (5 × 10 percent) on the down payment. At 50 times leverage (equivalent to a 2-percent down payment), a 10-percent change in the house price would result in a 500 percent (!) return on the down payment (50 × 10 percent).

You might be thinking that having high leverage and having your equity grow substantially over time is a great thing, and it is. Housing has been a huge source of wealth creation for millions of families all over the world. Borrowing to buy a home has both provided them with safe, comfortable places to live and built significant fortunes.

> Borrowing to buy a home has destroyed huge amounts of wealth and put families out of their homes, and leverage is the main reason.

But borrowing to buy a home has also destroyed huge amounts of wealth and put families out of their homes too, and it's the leverage that is the main reason. Here's why. If house prices go down, the decline in house price still gets leveraged by the mortgage borrowed. Back to Jen's situation: She bought her $300,000 home with a $30,000 down payment and a $270,000 mortgage. Now let's imagine what would happen if, instead of the house going up, it went down in value. What might that look like?

A 1-percent decline in the price of Jen's house would result in a 10-percent decline in the value of her investment. Her $300,000 house would decline 1 percent to $297,000 ($300,000 × (100 percent – 1 percent)), and her down payment investment would be worth $27,000 ($297,000 – $270,00), or 10-percent less than the amount she invested in her down payment.

And the bigger the decline in the house price, the worse the result. A 5-percent decline in the house price would result in a 50-percent decline in the value of Jen's down payment to $15,000 ($300,000 × (100 percent – 5 percent) = $285,000; $285,000 – $270,000 = $15,000), or half of her original investment (10 × –5 percent = –50 percent).

A 10-percent decline in the price of Jen's house would result in a complete loss of her original investment — a 100-percent decline.

But it doesn't stop there.

If Jen's house price were to decline 15 percent, her house would be worth $255,000 ($300,000 × (100 percent – 15 percent)). That's a big problem for Jen because she still owes $270,000 on her mortgage. That means that, if Jen wants to move, she could sell her house for $255,000, which she could use to pay off some of her mortgage, but she would need another $15,000 of savings to completely pay off the mortgage.

It took Jen quite a bit of effort to save up her initial down payment of $30,000. Since she bought her home, she hasn't been able to save any more money, what with all of her spare money going to mortgage payments, repairs to the house, and property taxes. So, for Jen, it looks like she can't afford to move. That could be a real problem if she lost her job or needed to move somewhere else. Even if she wanted to go back to renting and move to a smaller house, she'd be deeply in debt.

⊙   ⊙   ⊙

Leverage makes everything *more*. It makes good things even better and bad things even worse. Looking at the house price returns over the past twenty-five years, it becomes a little clearer how housing has come to be viewed as a great investment. An average price increase of 4 percent translates to a 40-percent rate of return on equity for a homeowner with a 10-percent down payment. This leverage is greatest in the first few years of a mortgage, before much has been repaid, giving house price changes the highest impact on changes to the value of equity in a home in the first few years after buying. Buyers with small down payments really need house prices to go up in the first few years, or at least stay flat, or else they run the risk of the house being worth less than the mortgage.

Over the last twenty-five years, most of the housing in most of Canada's major markets has risen. As a result, the power of leverage has made owning a home over the last twenty-five years look a lot better than what we covered in the last chapter.

But there's an aspect of this rise that isn't usually considered, one with very negative consequences. While most homeowners talk about how great an investment their house has been, what's usually not mentioned (or even considered when calculating the real value of homes as investments) is all the payments made on the mortgage. Each one slowly reduces the mortgage balance, until eventually it's paid off. It's easy to forget all those payments and ignore the fact that all of those hundreds of mortgage payments ended up not only repaying the entire balance of the mortgage taken out to buy their home, but also paying tens and even hundreds of thousands of dollars of interest.

> Part of the reason houses are so expensive in Canada is that our mortgage industry has made it easier to borrow with higher and higher leverage.

## MORTGAGE MARKETS MAKE HOUSING MORE EXPENSIVE

Ironically, part of the reason houses are so expensive in Canada is that our mortgage industry has made it easier and easier to borrow, and easier to borrow with higher and higher leverage. Making leverage available increases people's ability to pay higher prices for houses, and because of this, people are willing to pay more.

Imagine if everyone had to pay the whole amount in cash when they bought a house. It would take a lot longer for people to save up enough money to buy a house. More people would live in each house, and each house would probably be smaller. Children would live with their parents longer, and houses would cost a whole lot less.

We know this because mortgages haven't always been available, and they still aren't in a lot of countries. House prices were much lower before mortgages were available and are much lower in countries where mortgages aren't available.

Back in 2005, my wife, Natalie, and I went on vacation to Brazil. It was a fabulous trip, and we loved all of the places we went, from Rio de Janeiro, to Buzios, to Iguazu Falls, and places in between.

Being a property-obsessed real estate analyst, before we went I'd read about the housing market in Brazil. I learned that it was pretty underdeveloped. The houses themselves were generally not very sophisticated in terms of construction and design, and the banking system hadn't developed enough to make mortgages available to the general public. If you wanted a mortgage so you could buy a house, there was a small private market for mortgages. Because the government hadn't been actively promoting home ownership through housing policy, these private lenders were taking all of the risk themselves when they lent out money through mortgages, and so they demanded very high interest rates on the mortgages they did extend.

Further restricting the housing market in Brazil is the poverty of many of its residents and the poor quality of much of the country's housing stock. More than 10 million Brazilians live in what are called *favelas* — the Brazilian term for a slum. Rio and Brazil's other cities and large towns all have large slums where poor residents live in very small, crudely constructed houses they've built themselves. Many of the residents of the *favelas* don't own their homes — in fact, no one really owns them.

Despite the problems with the poverty of many Brazilians, the poor quality of much of the country's housing stock, and the lack of government support for home ownership, I had heard that there was a mortgage market starting to take shape. I was interested in learning more about how Brazil's housing market worked, and one day I found my opportunity when Natalie and I hired a taxi driver to take us around Rio to all of the notable sites. As we drove through the city, we chatted with our driver, who fortunately enough spoke English.

I asked him if he happened to own his own home. He lit up immediately, beaming with pride as he told us about the home he had bought for his family. Knowing the mortgage market wasn't well developed, and having heard interest rates were high, I asked him what interest rate he was paying on his mortgage.

What he said surprised me. He told me that he was paying 6 percent. It surprised me because, although I wasn't a homeowner, I knew that five-year mortgage rates in Canada were about 6 percent at that time.

That got me wondering if I'd been mistaken or had misunderstood the things I'd been reading about Brazil's mortgage market. Maybe the market was more developed than I thought.

A few minutes later it was all cleared up. Our driver was telling me that he had compared a couple of other lenders before he took out his mortgage, and that the other two were offering higher interest rates of 7 percent *per month*.

I was shocked. My new friend had told me the monthly interest rate on his mortgage, not the annual rate. That meant that he was paying 72-percent interest per year!

As much as I was shocked by this revelation, I was even more shocked that our driver was so enthusiastic about having a house.

I have no idea where our driver is today, but if he held on to his house from 2005, he probably has done quite well on his decision to buy. While there isn't good data prior to 2010, Brazilian house prices have risen sharply over the past decade, up more than 90 percent since 2010, when the Fundação Instituto de Pesquisas Econômicas (Institute of Economic Research) began tracking Brazilian house prices.

As it turns out, I was right about the beginnings of a mortgage market taking shape in 2005. The total mortgages volume in Brazil had nearly tripled in value by 2005, to R$4.8 billion from R$1.8 billion just three years earlier in 2002 (per the Central Bank of Brazil and the Brazilian Association of Real Estate Loans and Savings Companies). That's a lot of growth in only three years, but it was just the beginning. By the time lending had peaked in 2014, when the country entered a recession, the value of mortgages had grown to R$112.9 billion, or about sixty-three times the amount lent in 2002. The number of loans also increased sharply, from 29,000 to over 538,000. There had been an increase of 17 times the number of loans.

A part of the reason for this strong growth of mortgage debt was the development of pro–home ownership policies by the government. Included amongst these was the My Home My Life program, launched in 2009, that focused on increasing the availability of thirty-year mortgages and undertook the construction of over 3 million subsidized houses for low-income Brazilians.

Ironically, one of the major effects of the development of mortgage markets and pro–home ownership policies, both of which are developed to improve access to housing, is to inflate the price of housing (and ultimately create more volatility). The presence of a well-developed mortgage market gives all potential homeowners the ability to borrow a lot more, allowing them to pay more for housing. While we don't have good data on how house prices performed prior to 2010, the average amount of a new mortgage in Brazil rose from R$61,000 in 2002 to R$210,000 by 2014, more than tripling the average loan size. With each of these mortgages used to buy property, it would be hard to imagine that house prices didn't rise sharply over this period.

◎   ◎   ◎

Leverage amplifies returns. The more leverage, the more amplified the return. In the investment world, the best time to use high leverage is when the price of an investment is very low and beginning to rise. As prices rise, investors see returns leveraged or amplified to better and better returns. It's a glorious thing when it works well.

> The worst time to use leverage is when prices are very high and when everyone else is using leverage too.

Conversely, the worst time to use leverage is when prices are very high and when everyone else is using leverage too. That's because when other potential buyers have borrowed as much as possible, they can't buy any more. If prices fall, the losses are amplified, and everyone holding the investment loses more and more as the price declines. Levered buyers get hit the worst and can lose not only their equity, but also the money they borrowed, digging a deep financial hole.

Today Canadians pay 7 times the average gross family income to buy homes. That's a very high price, by historical standards.

While house prices are high by historical standards, Canadians have also borrowed significantly more today as a percentage of income than at any time in the past twenty-five years, and notably significantly more than Americans borrowed at the peak of the run-up to the 2008/2009 credit crisis.

A large mortgage for first-time homebuyers in Canada today can consume a huge portion of after-tax income. The combination of high prices, high leverage, and a high share of after-tax income dedicated to making mortgage payments doesn't leave much room for error.

## Canadian Home Price to Household Income

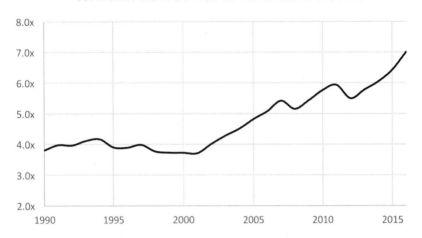

Source: CREA, CMHC.

## Household Debt as a % of Income

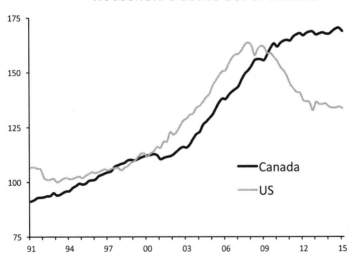

Source: Statistics Canada, Federal Reserve Board.

# CHAPTER 12

## Beyond Weak Returns, Housing Is Just a Terrible Investment

In Chapter 8 we looked at the numbers. Housing hasn't been a home run investment in Canada over the past few decades, even though Canada has seen very good house price increases, so the numbers don't look too good.

Things look even worse when you compare the investment characteristics of buying stocks or an index of stocks to a principal residence. I'm not talking about the returns. Ask any professional about what makes a good investment, and returns will be only a small part of the answer you get. A lot of other factors influence the investment decisions of professional investors.

The investment characteristics of all investments include liquidity, fungibility (that's not a typo), whether the investment is one you can bet for *and* against (long/short investible), transaction costs, scalability, and personal and other lifestyle impacts, among others.

On all of these measures, homes fall hugely short of stocks, bonds, mutual funds and index funds, and even investments in income-producing properties (as distinct from owner-occupied homes) on some measures.

For instance, liquidity: Stock indices can be traded nearly every weekday, all year long between 9:30 a.m. and 4:00 p.m., in huge amounts. Once you've traded the stock, it usually takes three business days for a trade to "settle" — for the actual stock to land in your account.

In contrast, it can take weeks and months, and even years, to sell houses. Once a sale is agreed to, it usually take three months to close (or "settle").

Making this even worse, more than half of all sales occur in the spring, meaning that buying and selling houses is not only very slow, but also very seasonal. (Renters may be locked into a lease, but once the lease is expired the renter can just move out — something that is easier and definitely cheaper than selling a home.)

Part of the reason it takes a whole lot longer to sell houses than other investments is because houses aren't fungible. "Fungible" is a term that means things are identical and completely interchangeable. Stocks are fungible because every share of stock in a company is exactly the same. They are indistinguishable from each other. So are loonies and toonies — they're all worth exactly the same amount and are completely interchangeable.

> More than half of all home sales occur in the spring, making buying and selling houses not only very slow, but also very seasonal.

Houses, in contrast, are entirely unique — every one of them! The side of the street a house is on needs to be taken into account. And how many square feet it has. Is there a bathroom on the main floor? Even in condominium complexes, where the floor plans and even the interior finishes could be exactly the same, each home is different: a different elevation or floor, a different view out the window.

Generally speaking, the older a neighbourhood, condominium building, or other housing development, the less alike homes become. Over time, homes get old and tired. Renovations are made, and gradually, over time, similar houses begin to differ more and more.

Another appealing investment characteristic found in stocks and bonds, but not in housing, is the ability to "short" an investment. Shorting a stock, bond, or index is betting that prices will fall. The technical mechanism for shorting works like this: An investor "borrows" stock held by another investor and then sells it into the market. The investor has now locked in a sale price and has promised to repurchase the stock at a later time and return it to the investor they borrowed it from. Later, they buy back that stock in the market, hopefully at a lower price, and return it to the original owner. In this way, investors can not only bet on the price of an investment going up, by buying and then selling an investment later at a higher price they can also bet on it going down.

Despite numerous attempts by investment banks and financial innovators, there has been no successful way developed for investors to bet directly against house prices. This lack of ability to short houses has the effect of creating an imbalanced market for house prices and tends to lead to bubble-like markets. With every person in the world requiring accommodation and no way for investors to effectively bet against house prices, the market is made up of only buyers of housing.

Then there are the transaction costs. If you bought a house for $500,000 and sold it five years later at the same price, you could easily pay $50,000 or more in transaction costs, as noted earlier. By comparison, Canadian discount brokerages will usually have a basic commission of less than $10 for most trades — including trades for more than $500,000 worth of stock, leaving the comparable purchase-and-sale combination at under $20 of transaction costs. That means the transaction costs on buying and selling a $500,000 house are 2,500 times more than the transaction costs of buying and selling $500,000 of stock, bonds, or mutual funds.

Let me say that again. The transaction costs on buying and selling houses are 2,500 times higher than buying and selling other common investments.

That alone should rule out buying a house from a pure investment perspective.

Another drawback of housing as an investment is the magnitude of the investment. Renters don't need to put all of their savings into the rent they pay, even if they're leasing an expensive house or apartment. But because homes are so expensive, costing hundreds of thousands of dollars nearly everywhere across the country, you can't just buy a little investment in a home — you have to make a large investment. Most other investments can be scaled to fit your needs: $500, $50,000, or $500,000, or almost anything in between. Homes are just sold in quantities of one, with prices in the hundreds of thousands of dollars. This is also pretty inconvenient in the sense that buying a home is something many people can't do with cash alone. They need to take on a significant amount of mortgage debt.

> Unlike homeowners, renters don't need to put all of their savings into the rent they pay, even if they're leasing an expensive house or apartment.

So, because of the large scale of the transaction, not only is a home purchase something you can't ease into over time, but also you are generally going to have to invest all of your personal wealth and your future savings in it (in the form of a mortgage), all at one point in time. The prospect of making such a concentrated, leveraged investment in a single asset would make most people run away in fear. Just try suggesting to a friend that they take all of the money they have in the world, then borrow ten times as much from a bank, and invest it all in a hot stock tip! Yet, for housing, it's so common and socially acceptable, people don't bat an eye.

The last major, and perhaps most damning aspect, of looking at buying a home as an investment is the deeply personal entwinement homes have with our lives.

Professional investors spend their entire careers trying to eliminate things that interfere with making good investment decisions. They deal with all sorts of behavioural challenges, like confirmation biases (paying more attention to facts that support your conclusion), reference points and anchoring (putting too much importance on the first facts learned about a topic), and the recency effect (remembering more readily recent information than older information), all of which are psychological tendencies that contribute to bad investment decision-making.

But they never have to deal with timing the purchase or sale of a specific investment based on their young child's school year or the desire to maintain friendships and continue to be a part of a local community. They never have to try to avoid the disruption of moving when life is busy: cleaning out your closets and storage areas before listing your house, leaving your home during real estate agent open houses, packing up all of your belongings ahead of a move, finding and arranging new accommodations, and all of the other complications that make moving homes a challenging task.

It really doesn't get any more personal than your home. Where you live is so inextricably linked to your friends, family, schools, and community, it's impossible to make a housing decision without considering the potentially dramatic impact a change could have on all parts of your life. That is a terrible condition to attach to an investment.

From a pure investment perspective, housing fails to offer any of the convenient and appealing features of stocks, bonds, and other common investments. It's just a plain lousy investment. Any other investment with these characteristics would have to offer extraordinary return prospects for an investor to even look twice.

# CHAPTER 13

## Investment Creep

There's another big problem with housing as an investment. It's called investment creep.

Think about the last time you went shopping for one thing and found yourself with a better, more expensive version of the thing you originally were looking for. You basically let yourself be up-sold into buying a more luxurious version of what you were planning to get. The reason for your purchase didn't need to be the pitch of a slick sales rep. It could have been an ad you saw weeks or months earlier that diverted your eye toward your ultimate purchase. It could have been a feature sheet that showed much better value for the price, once you compared it to what you had been planning to buy. Maybe the design was more aesthetically pleasing — even sexy! Or it could have been a special sale on the pricier product.

It's easy. Really easy. And that's why we do it.

You're looking to get a car, because you don't have one, or the one you have is getting old/sounding rough/not big enough/too big/ugly. Do you buy it new? Do you buy it used? Do you get the optional leather seats? Power windows?

If you're like most of us, you start out with an idea of what you need and want. Then you look for a place to get what you need. It doesn't matter if you're the type that spends weeks and weeks analyzing your options, comparison shopping, and polling people you know about how they like their cars, or the type that drives to the closest showroom and talks it out with a salesperson, or anything in between.

Odds are that the car you end up getting is a little more expensive and a little more impressive than what you were thinking of when you started.

And why not? The leather will hold up better. It wipes clean, while upholstery would stain. The newer model has a higher safety rating. The model up has more horsepower, which is really a safety feature, when you think about it.

The fact is, most things we buy are so well marketed that they aren't just a car or a fridge or a watch. They've become extensions of our identity. A lot of people believe the watch you wear says something about who you are. A Swatch or a Timex could be sporty, thrifty, and practical. An expensive, hand-crafted Swiss watch from TAG Heuer or Rolex says that you're successful, you care about your appearance, and you're willing to spend money on the finer things in life.

The point is that we live in a world saturated with marketing and materialism, and it's almost impossible to remain immune to the psychology of materialism and the idea of "keeping up with the Joneses."

Now apply that thinking to the most expensive thing you could ever buy (or rent!). The thing that forms the stage on which we all live out our daily lives. The most personal and private space we have and, at the same time, for many people the most prominent manifestation of who we want the world to see us as. And that leads to all sorts of strange decisions that people might not otherwise make, particularly when you contrast modern housing features with the necessities we require from housing, like a six-burner Wolf range costing 20 times the most basic electric stove available.

> When buying a home, it's easy to lose track of the difference between our housing needs and our housing wants. This is where investment creep comes in.

It's easy to lose track of the difference between our housing needs and our desires for housing, which include all sorts of finishes, features, and spaces. There is no thick black line separating the needs from the wants, just a grey continuum of blurring between what is necessary and what is desirable.

This is where investment creep comes in.

Investment creep will sneak up on you in the kitchen. There you are, in the kitchen of a home for sale. You might be with your spouse or boyfriend, a best friend or parent, or you might be alone with your real estate agent.

You've got your budget and your wish list of must-have's and ideally's, and you're looking to buy. Inside of your head, or out loud with your partner or advisor, the conversation will bounce back and forth from the first place you saw the day before to the one you saw that morning to the one you're standing in, and how each stack up against your list.

House A had a great kitchen but a terrible view. House B fit your budget perfectly, but the kitchen and bathrooms needed updating. The kitchen you're standing in has it all, but it's just out of reach from a budget perspective.

It's at this moment that you fall victim to investment creep. That's the term I use for what happens when a person looking for housing justifies paying more than they planned, or would otherwise consider, on the basis that it's an investment and it should go up in value over time.

The thinking and justification can go along a number of different lines:

- Houses go up in value, so the more we spend, the bigger the gains will be!
- It's an investment in our lifestyle, and it has the added benefit that it will go up in value.
- It can cost a lot to move, so if we spend more this time, we won't have to move again, and we're really saving money on a future move.
- This beautiful house is already "done," so we won't have to do any renovations, which always cost more than you expect and are a huge amount of work and a disruption to everyday life.

All of these arguments have some truth to them. But none of them would stand up to the scrutiny of a professional investor.

Probably the biggest error homebuyers fall victim to through investment creep is failing to acknowledge the total and ongoing costs of a home and overspending on a home that looks and feels great. A new kitchen, nice bathrooms, a guest bedroom for when friends and family want to come and visit ... all very nice things to have — if you can afford them.

At the moment you are making your decision, the person standing beside you is probably a real estate agent. They are incentivized to see you buy, and if it's a competitive market, that means being the highest bidder. The other person who you've been talking to a lot is the mortgage broker or banker who wants to lend you money, the more the better.

Ironically, as you stand in this gorgeous kitchen, you don't think about how the performance of a house as an investment is inversely related to the features it might offer. Said another way, the newest, biggest, shiniest, and most expensive house on the street has more of its value contained in the house, rather than the land, than any other house on the street. That means that more of the investment made in that house will go down in value than it will for any other house on the street.

The oldest, smallest, and most tired house on the street will have the least value tied up in the house and the highest portion tied up in the land. Which is what should go up in value over time, making the small, old, and even dumpy house a better investment, from a purely financial perspective.

Nevertheless, if you ask any real estate agent what the most common justification for going over budget on a home purchase is, it's investment creep. They won't call it that, but it's the same idea.

Understanding the mix of investment (land) and consumption (buildings) in buying a home can help you

Home buying needs to be seen for what it really is: an investment in land plus consumption of the glamorous building that has been erected on that piece of land.

resist the pull of investment creep. But it's not at all easy. Human nature says we'll rationalize overspending on housing by arranging a series of facts and opinions that support the outcome we most want to believe is best.

Am I suggesting that we should all live in the smallest, most tired and rundown home, essentially the "tear-down" house on the street? Absolutely not. But home buying needs to be seen for what it really is: an investment in land plus consumption of the glamorous building that has been erected on that piece of land.

How much consumption? To figure this out, we can figure out land value by looking for nearby homes on similar-sized lots that were recently sold and subsequently torn down. The difference between that price and what a homebuyer pays for a nearby home is what they are paying for the building. And that is the consumption portion of the purchase price.

The value of a building doesn't go away in a year or even over the course of a decade or more. But it goes down, and the more building you have, the less land value you have. The erosion of value of a building is a particularly dangerous thing because it's not something you can see or monitor on a month-to-month or year-to-year basis. The deterioration of value of a home takes place silently and is only apparent once a home is sold. It can be extremely expensive. With such a personal thing as buying a home, it's easy to mistake consumption for investment.

## STOP INVESTMENT CREEP COLD

Fortunately, there is a 100-percent bullet-proof solution to the problem of investment creep: renting! One of the best things about renting is that there can be no investment creep. Because there is clearly no investment being made, renters are forced to see rent for what it is — a consumption item. That makes it easier to see the difference between what they need and what they want. This leads to a much more transparent decision to make about where to live. It's a simple, straightforward arrangement in which rent is paid for the service of providing housing. There is no confusion about what part of the housing cost is an expense versus an investment. Renters don't have to wonder whether house prices are cheap or expensive or whether they'll go up or down — it doesn't matter to them.

> In renting, there can be no investment creep, so renters have an easier time telling the difference between what they need and want.

I've met a few people who have been particularly enlightened about housing. They generally work in the real estate industry, and these people are renters by choice. The thing that makes them so unique is that, as renters, they have chosen to pay for renovations and improvements to the rented homes they live in.

Imagine that. They are paying to renovate the kitchen or the bathrooms (or any part, for that matter) of their landlord's house.

Why would they do that? Well, they tell me a few reasons. First, they like the place they are living in, it's a hassle to move, and the only thing they aren't happy with is the kitchen or bathroom or whatever. They also tell me that they like the idea of the discipline that comes with knowing that the renovation they are paying for is in no way a financial investment, but purely a consumption item.

Finally, these enlightened renters generally made an agreement with their landlord that the rents won't change significantly for a few years and that, if they leave the home for any reason in the next few years, the landlord will pay them a portion of the cost of the renovation. In one case, the agreement was that if the tenant left in the first year, the landlord would reimburse them 50 percent of the cost of the renovation, dropping to 35 percent in the second year and 20 percent if they left in years three or four.

Pretty interesting thinking, eh? It kind of turns the tables on the idea that as a tenant you have no control over what improvements are made to your place.

One last thing about these people: They are very wealthy. They could have easily bought their homes and paid with cash, but they chose not to.

Back to investment creep. What's insidious about investment creep is that it only occurs in purchases that have elements of investment and consumption, the largest of which is our housing. That's what makes it particularly dangerous and potentially damaging to our financial health.

There are other places it can occur. Vintage car collections. Antiques. Fine wines. Even stamp collections and baseball cards. If you collect any of these kinds of assets, you'll know that the desire to own the car of your dreams or the finest collectibles or that prized possession can be powerful. But most of these assets represent a small portion of our wealth, and people seem to have a much easier time exercising restraint in buying collectible items.

Sometimes spouses help those of us who are collectors exercise that restraint, although that is often not the case in housing decisions. A home can be universally appealing. As we decide what type of home we'll live in, we're faced with thoughts about what our friends will think of this house, what it says about our success, what schools our kids will attend, and how committed we are to providing the best for ourselves and our families. It's easy to see how people buy into the story that friends, family, and the remainder of the cheerleading squad promoting home ownership (including realtors) are selling when they tell you, "Go for it — it's an investment!"

# CHAPTER 14

## Everyone Wins When You Buy a Home (Except Maybe You!)

There's a very good reason we get a lot of advice that says we should buy a home: A lot of people stand to benefit from that kind of advice and from adding another person to the cult of "Why Rent When You Can Buy?" There are a lot of people who will try to persuade you to buy a home or to sell the home you own and buy another home, even if it might be a better idea for you to rent instead. In the next two chapters, I'll introduce you to the main players in this group. Now, I'm not suggesting that they're bad people; in fact, most of them want the best for you. But, as we'll see, they all stand to benefit if you buy.

The first line of advisors for most housing decisions is friends and family, and, more often than not, it's our parents who we look to first. I think that's natural. By the time we're preparing to make our first housing decisions, we've been living our lives on the housing stage that our parents set with their housing decisions.

Our parents have also generally been a go-to source for all sorts of advice by that point in our lives, from how to wash our hands to how to ride a bike to how to read and use proper manners (whether we took that advice or not). On top of their roles as a source of general advice, parents tend to like to give housing advice in particular because they intuitively know that housing decisions are some of the biggest decisions we'll ever have to make, and they want us to make good decisions about the important things in life.

Odds are that the best qualification most parents have for providing advice on housing is having bought and owned a house, or possibly more than one. After all, 70 percent of Canadians are homeowners, and ownership is even higher among parents. That's not a very good qualification at all.

If it were, anyone who has bought a car is a car expert. Anyone who has bought a stock is a financial wizard. I've spent thousands of hours flying all over the place on commercial airline flights. Am I an expert? Not a single airline has offered me a job as a pilot!

In reality, having bought and sold a house means that a person knows more about buying and selling houses than someone who has never bought or sold. But that is a long way from being an expert.

> Odds are that the best qualification most parents have for providing advice on housing is having bought and owned a house. That's not a very good qualification at all.

Your parents likely believe they've made good housing decisions. They will definitely believe they've made good housing decisions if they bought a home and it went up in value. Even if they bought a home that went down in value, they likely believe it was still a good housing decision — they just need to wait for the market to come back.

That's natural. It happens all the time in the investment world. There are even lots of different psychology terms for the various ways people convince themselves they've made good decisions in the face of evidence to the contrary: cognitive dissonance, familiarity bias, reference points and anchoring, the law of small numbers, the endowment effect, status quo bias, mental accounting, and overconfidence, among others. In fact, the study of investor psychology and its effects on investment decision-making is one of the fastest growing areas of study in the financial world, and it's called behavioural finance.

Most of the time, parents will recommend that you buy a house. Why would they do this? Whether they've made good or bad housing decisions, recommending that you buy a house makes them feel better for four good reasons:

- It affirms their decision to buy a house. This is something that occurs at a very basic, subconscious level. It's a natural psychological bias. It's what marketers exploit to get us to buy things. We all want to be a part of a group. With housing, it's easier to see this dynamic demonstrated with young people right after they have just bought a house (though the feeling never goes away). They're nervous and uncomfortable about having just made the biggest purchase of their lives, and they'd feel a lot better if you and everyone you know also bought a house. They'll even tell you so: "We're so excited. The house/neighbourhood/backyard/local restaurant is so great! You guys should buy the house down the street — it's for sale, you know!"

- Having more buyers helps house prices go higher. If you buy, that's one more person choosing ownership over renting, and even though you're just one person or family, there are lots of cult members out there. This one is also generally a subconscious and instinctual feeling. It's also more about not recommending that their children choose to rent, which would be contrary to their own choices and perceived success in housing.
- It means their kids won't go through their entire lives without having accumulated a dollar of savings. That's because buying a home means that eventually their kids will have accumulated some savings once they have paid off a mortgage. Right or wrong, parents often see their kids as less responsible than they are, and that's mainly because parents are older and more mature (most of the time) than kids. And, for a lot of parents, the only savings they've ever accumulated is the equity in their home, after having paid off their mortgage. As it turns out, buying a home is an okay savings program, but not a great one (more on this later). But for parents giving advice to their children, any savings program is better than no savings program. Home ownership is the most well-known and popular savings program around. It's tough to blame parents for this one — there's good merit in the idea.
- A mortgage will make you grow up — and parents like anything that will make their kids more responsible! Anyone who's ever had a mortgage knows that the day you take a mortgage, you start to look at the world a little differently. You gain respect for property. Your attendance record at work improves, even if it was good to begin with. And you become part of a community.

It might be hard to think about the above four points as your parents "winning," but it certainly helps explain the bias they might have toward suggesting you buy rather than rent. Generally speaking, your parents don't necessarily think about any of these four points. They just feel good about telling their kids to buy homes.

The same can be said for other family members and friends, who are also driven by the same ideas when they recommend buying a house. They can just feel at some subconscious level that buying a house will be good for you. In many cases they're right — it can do a lot of good things for you. But it might not be the absolute best thing for you.

While friends and family are key members of the push to buy houses, the people who work in the housing industry are the focused professionals in the business of selling houses and promoting home ownership: real estate agents, mortgage brokers, and lenders. All people who get paid when houses are bought and sold. The more the house costs, the more they get paid.

For these professionals, the only thing better for them financially than someone buying a house is someone buying and selling several houses. That's not to say they don't genuinely care about their customers and clients or that they wouldn't do the "right thing" for them. It's just fact: Housing professionals get paid more when more homes sell and when they sell for higher and higher prices. Real estate agents get paid directly each time a house is bought and sold. Banks make money by making mortgage loans.

Let's look at some of the strategies they use. Like any other group of professionals might do, this group uses marketing and promotion strategies to drive more business — more moves and more mortgages. Some of these strategies and concepts are probably familiar to you.

## THE STARTER HOME

The idea of a starter home is one marketing angle created by the housing industry to get people into home ownership. The idea is pretty simple: If you aren't ready to make the leap into a home that will make sense for five or ten years, you can jump into the market early by buying a "starter home" that allows you to get "into" the market a couple years earlier than you otherwise would have.

Implicit in the idea of the starter home is that the buyer would live in the house for only a couple years before moving up to a larger and more permanent home that better fits their needs. Also implicit in this idea is that the housing market would see prices rise during that few years of starter-home ownership. Otherwise, there would be no need to get into the market sooner.

The starter-home pitch often relies on fear as a motivator: If you don't get in now, you might not be able to afford to get in later, once prices go up. Fear is a powerful motivator. But often, using this pressure tactic can drive irrational fear and irrational actions. The thought of never being able to afford to buy a house because house prices have risen so quickly you can never catch up is irrational. So is buying a house to get into the market.

With a starter-home strategy, the price of a house must rise by at least 10 percent (but usually more) for a buyer to break even on the purchase of a starter home over the, say, two years they stay in the starter home. The math gets better as the length of ownership increases, if prices continue to rise, but the whole concept never gets compelling.

Let's assume a couple, Tim and Jessica, are renting a place for $1,100 a month. Feeling badly about "throwing their money away" on rent and fearing that if they don't get into the market now they might never be able to get in if prices rise, they decide to buy a starter home. So they take their $50,000 of savings and use it as a down payment to buy a $250,000 house:

| | |
|---|---|
| Purchase price: | $250,000 |
| Land transfer tax (Ontario): | $2,225 |
| Legal and moving costs: | $2,000 |
| Down payment: | $50,000 |
| Mortgage: | $204,225 |

Two years later, they sell their home at a price 7-percent higher. While they owned it, they paid $1,074 per month on the mortgage (pretty much what they were paying in rent). That totals $25,776, including $9,952 of principal payments over the two years, reducing the mortgage balance. They also paid $5,000 in total property taxes (2 years × $2,500):

| | |
|---|---|
| Sale price: | $267,500 |
| Brokerage fees (5 percent): | $13,375 |
| Legal and moving costs: | $2,000 |
| Mortgage: | $196,913 |
| Net sale proceeds: | $56,143 |

The sale proceeds of $56,143 compared to the initial $50,000 down payment looks pretty good. Except that the couple paid $5,000 of property taxes, which they weren't paying when they were renting.

So, after all the effort of moving, and netting out the cost of the added property taxes, the couple ended up with $51,143 ($56,143 less the $5,000 of added property taxes) from a $50,000 investment over a two-year period. That equates to about a 1.1-percent return per year. We've also assumed nothing goes wrong with the house and that there is no maintenance cost.

History suggests that the likelihood of a home sold after just two years working out in favour of the buyer is extremely low. Had the house price instead remained unchanged, Tim and Jessica would be left with just $38,337, for a loss of 23 percent of their down payment (and they would have paid $5,000 in property taxes!). The math only gets worse if the house goes down in value. A high price for getting "into" the market.

If they had instead kept their $50,000 in a bank account paying 2 percent interest, after two years it would have grown to $52,020. Add to that the $5,000 of property taxes they wouldn't have had to pay as renters and the $50,000 of savings would have grown to $57,020, for a total increase of 14 percent. And Tim and Jessica's money would never have been at risk sitting in a bank account.

Of course, not everyone loses with a starter-home purchase. Some people are lucky enough to have house prices rise rapidly, and others end up staying in their homes longer than planned — long enough to see a real rise in the value of their home. After three full years of the home rising in value by 3.5 percent, the annual return on the original $50,000 rises to 8 percent, reaching nearly 13 percent by year seven. Using a lot of leverage (Tim and Jessica had five times leverage on their purchase) works if house prices go up and if homeowners own for long enough. They just have to wait a few years before seeing any gains.

However, the real estate agent who gets you into the market by helping you buy a starter home always wins — from day one! They will most likely get paid twice: once to buy and once to sell that starter home. In the previous example, 50 percent of the brokerage fees on each of the purchase and sale transactions (agents usually split the fee of approximately 5 percent between the agent representing the buyer and the one representing the seller) amounts to $12,937.50 (or $12,500, should the price not go up). That definitely benefits the real estate agent. Agents usually get to keep more than 25 percent of the total commission on a transaction after splitting it between the two agents (one for buyer, one for seller) and paying their brokerage company a share. So it's not surprising that both the concept of a starter home and the use of fear in its promotion are common in the real estate industry. In fact, the use of fear as a selling tool is common across many sales professions.

## THE PROPERTY LADDER

The property ladder is another one of these concepts, and it's basically an extension of the starter home. The idea is that people can work their way up from a starter home to an intermediate home to a trophy home, all by making savvy trades from house to house. The strategy suggests that a savvy homebuyer can essentially leverage a small investment into something much bigger, apparently with little more than good timing and a good real estate agent.

On the surface, this concept seems very compelling. You pay one down payment on your first home. That house goes up in value. You roll that into a larger down payment on a larger, more expensive house. And someday you might find yourself in your very own dream home.

Another way to describe that strategy is doubling down on high-leverage bets. You'll find it very common at casinos. That doesn't always work out so well.

At its best, the property ladder is an aggressive, high-leverage strategy of investing in relatively stable assets. At its worst, the property ladder is a thinly disguised marketing and sales pitch to encourage people to take on a series of high-risk transactions, wagering both their financial and personal housing arrangements, designed to generate big transaction fees and stimulate demand to push house prices higher.

The truth is probably somewhere in the middle.

With the property ladder, it is clearly the real estate agent who benefits most. It allows them to recommend buying a house earlier than a potential buyer might otherwise. It also means the agent has a pretty good chance of handling the purchase and sale of not just your starter home, but of maybe several homes. The math works out very well in favour of the agent and only works for the buyer if house prices rise at high rates.

## HOUSE FLIPPING

Another marketing strategy is the concept of flipping homes. This is when an "investor" buys a home and completes a quick and mostly cosmetic renovation, only to immediately sell the house.

This practice has been glamorized through a number of popular TV shows, like *Flip This House*, *The Big Flip*, and *Flipping Out*. It makes for good TV: the promise of windfall gains from just a few short weeks of hard work. Doing something that's interesting and different.

Again, with this strategy, it's the real estate agents who benefit the most. An agent can collect two commissions on the same house, assuming they help to both buy and later sell the same house over a short period of time (weeks to months).

> Despite how clearly agents and lenders are incentivized to encourage people to buy and sell, these professionals are included in the group most people look to for advice on housing.

The flipper takes on a lot of risk: risk of finding a leaky foundation, hidden asbestos, improper electrical wiring, or any number of other surprises that could cost thousands of dollars, not to mention the risk that the market could soften. These risks carry the potential to wipe out any potential profits. In contrast, the agent takes on virtually no risk and in most cases can make more than the flippers themselves. For an agent, a client who flips houses is a dream client, especially those who buy and sell several homes a year.

Despite all of the above examples that demonstrate how clearly agents and lenders are incentivized to encourage people to buy (and sell) houses, remarkably, real estate agents and mortgage professionals are included in the group most people look to for advice on housing.

I'll make a fine point here: Agents and mortgage professionals can be excellent advisors — for the right things. Those things are pretty specific. Agents are great resources for finding the right house in the right neighbourhood and at the right price. They can help you find a home for rent or a home for sale. Mortgage professionals are great advisors on what options are available for financing the purchase of a home.

What they're not particularly good at advising on is what type of housing is right for a given person. These advisors specialize in owned housing, not rental, and not in helping people make the decision of whether renting or buying is right for a given person. That's a decision that needs to be made before agents and mortgage professionals can be helpful.

Clearly, most of the people we look to for advice on housing are biased toward home ownership.

There's someone else who wants you to buy a house. Here's the beginning of a speech given by one of the leaders of this group:

> *Thank you, all. Thanks, for coming. Well, thanks for the warm welcome. Thank you for being here today. I appreciate your attendance to this very important conference. You see, we want everybody in America to own their own home. That's what we want. This is — An ownership society is a compassionate society.*

It shouldn't surprise you to learn that the speech in question was delivered by George W. Bush in 2002 at a Department of Housing and Urban Development conference. No less than the former president of the United States wants you to buy a home! And that's just the tip of the iceberg. Governments all around the world are working hard to get you to buy a house. When you do, they win big time.

Agents can help you find a home for rent or a home for sale, but they're not particularly good at helping people decide whether renting or buying is right for them.

# CHAPTER 15

## Big Brother Wants You to Buy a House

Sounds menacing. Sounds like a conspiracy theory. Depending on how you look at it, it's fair to say governments around the world are conspiring to get people to buy houses.

Let's get back to that speech from 2002. In that speech, Bush announced a target of making 5.5 million more minority families into homeowners by the end of the decade (2010). He also announced $2 billion of tax credits for homebuilders to promote construction of affordable housing, as well as a new fund, called the American Dream Downpayment Initiative, created to grant down payments to Americans having difficulty overcoming one of the largest hurdles to home ownership: saving up enough money for a down payment. Plus, a $55-million educational program to promote home ownership among minorities.

> *All of us here in America should believe, and I think we do, that we should be, as I mentioned, a nation of owners. Owning something is freedom, as far as I'm concerned. It's part of a free society. And ownership of a home helps bring stability to neighbourhoods. You own your home in a neighbourhood, you have more interest in how your neighbourhood feels, looks, whether it's safe or not. It brings pride to people, it's a part of an asset-based society. It helps people build up their own individual portfolio,*

*provides an opportunity, if need be, for a mom or a dad to leave something to their child. It's a part of … it's of being a … it's a part of … an important part of America.*

Clearly the U.S. government is very much in favour of home ownership. The Canadian government has been actively promoting home ownership, too, driving ownership rates higher ever since they started tracking the market.

And why shouldn't they be? When you buy a house, you instantly become a better citizen. You become more law-abiding and have better respect for property rights. You work toward building a better community, and that's not all. Once you buy a house, you'll work harder, save more money, and create jobs.

> There are many benefits to having a society of homeowners. It just might not be the best choice for you.

You can't blame the government. It all sounds pretty good, and the truth is that it actually is. There are many benefits to having a society of homeowners. It just might not be the best choice for you.

Not surprisingly, pro–home ownership policies are popular in almost all developed countries. Canada, the United States, Australia, Britain, France, Italy, Spain, Portugal, Greece, Japan, and many, many other nations have government agencies that are tasked with promoting home ownership. Here are just a few of those organizations:

## CANADA

- Canada Mortgage and Housing Corporation (CMHC)

## UNITED STATES

- Federal Housing Authority
- Department of Housing and Urban Development

- Federal National Mortgage Association (Fannie Mae)
- Government National Mortgage Association (Ginnie Mae)
- Federal Home Loan Mortgage Corporation (Freddie Mac)

## HONG KONG

- Hong Kong Housing Authority
- Home Ownership Scheme
- Sandwich Class Housing Scheme
- Hong Kong Housing Society

## SINGAPORE

- Housing and Development Board

## UNITED KINGDOM

- Department for Communities and Local Government
- Housing and Communities Agency

## FRANCE

- Fonds de garantie de l'accession sociale
- Habitation à loyer modéré

## AUSTRALIA

- Housing Affordability Fund

You might be asking why there are so many of these organizations. How much money gets spent every year by these organizations as they encourage home ownership in all these countries? CMHC has roughly $250 billion of assets, while the Department of Housing and Urban Development alone has an annual budget of nearly $50 billion. There are trillions of dollars of government money globally dedicated to home ownership.

That's a lot of money. It underscores how important increasing the rate of home ownership is to governments.

So let's talk about how home ownership helps a society and its people. There are many theories on how home ownership benefits a society. Most of them boil down to the idea that home ownership helps create a productive and disciplined society. Owning a home makes people more likely to work hard, stay employed, abide by the laws of the land, and generally behave in a predictable and manageable way. And I think there's something to most of these arguments.

We can group these ideas and arguments into three categories: quality of life, economic development, and social control.

## QUALITY OF LIFE: HOME OWNERSHIP IMPROVES LIVING STANDARDS

Housing is a basic human requirement. This concept was most clearly articulated by Abraham Maslow in 1943 in his seminal work, *A Theory of Human Motivation*. Maslow identified the priority of human needs, known as Maslow's Hierarchy of Needs, beginning with the most basic and progressing through to the most complex and sophisticated. The first group of needs includes physiological needs, like breathing, food, sleep, and — you guessed it — shelter. That is to say, housing is as important to human life as breathing, sleeping, and eating.

But it doesn't stop there. The next group up is safety, which includes security of property and shelter. Again, housing shows up as a very basic requirement of human life. There are good arguments to suggest quality of housing is a critical factor in the higher groups of human needs.

Home ownership creates a sense of community. Owning a home is a big commitment, and usually it provides a sense of permanency. It takes time to find a place so well suited that you want to buy it. Then it takes time to move, and it's expensive, so most people like to stay in a home for a while, longer than in a rented home. The longer you stay in one place, the more you get to know the neighbours. When you build friendships and relationships with your neighbours, you begin to care about them and look out for them. And that's the basis of community. By comparison, renting is much less of a financial commitment, usually doesn't last as long, and tends to generate less of a sense of community.

Home ownership supports family values. Owned homes are more work than rented housing, they're usually larger than rented housing, and in Canada they're often a little nicer than rented housing. All of those attributes make it likely that homeowners will spend more time at home, whether it's to mow the lawn, hang pictures, have friends over, or just enjoy the comfort of a nice home. The more time you spend at home, the more time you probably spend with family (unless you live alone) and the more likely it is that you'll get to know your neighbours and build a community. That's good for family values.

Home ownership is often a source of pride and satisfaction. As is the case with almost any shiny new thing you acquire, particularly very expensive things, a home that is bought immediately becomes a source of pride. Pride of ownership reflects the freedoms owning your own home provides: freedom to do what you like *in* the home, freedom to do what you like *to* the home (paint the hall, finish the basement, tear out the carpet, or whatever), and freedom to use the house anyway you'd like, including showing it off to friends and family — not the most modest of human behaviours, but still quite common.

Home ownership is associated with better health, and there are many academic studies that support this argument. If home ownership helps people become more responsible, build communities, and generally contribute more to society, it's not surprising it might improve health. Homeowners typically have mortgages that take decades to pay off. That's a long-term commitment requiring long-term thinking. The more long-term thinking a person does, the more likely they are to improve their lifestyle to better their health. But more basically, in the affordable housing arena, making the jump from homelessness to being housed has a dramatic positive effect on health.

## ECONOMIC DEVELOPMENT: A HOME-OWNING SOCIETY IS MORE PRODUCTIVE

Home ownership creates jobs. In the speech from 2002, Bush went on to attribute $256 billion of economic benefit to the stated goal of adding 5.5 million new homeowners. That worked out to about $46,500 of economic benefit for each additional renter who became a homeowner. The benefits and jobs come from direct construction jobs building houses, but also from related industries like appliance manufacturing, shipping and receiving, design and furnishing, maintenance, and services, among many others. Homeowners typically have more space and they fill that space up with more things than renters do.

Rising house prices can create wealth for homeowners, though often not as much wealth as many other investments, as we have seen. If house prices rise on a consistent basis, not only do homeowners benefit from the savings they accumulate through the principal payments made to pay down their mortgages, but the increasing value of their houses adds to those savings. This added wealth can be used in many ways, whether directly by the homeowner or even by their heirs, to invest in businesses, consumption, or even more real estate.

## SOCIAL CONTROL: A HOME-OWNING SOCIETY IS EASIER TO GOVERN

Home ownership leads to harder working, more productive societies. Once you have something to work for (your house) and an obligation (a mortgage) to make payments to keep that special something, you're more likely to work longer hours and take fewer sick (or not-so-sick) days. If you're old enough to have experienced this, you might not remember when it happened. It's a subtle change. But if you're like me, your behaviour began to change when you became a homeowner. Work or school attendance improved. You began planning for things in advance. You became generally more reliable.

Home ownership encourages mutual respect for property. Once you own that special something, you're proud of it and you want to protect it. That tends to create an understanding among homeowners of how they would like others to treat their belongings and, in turn, how they tend to treat the belongings of others.

Home ownership reduces crime. Once you have a home, a mortgage, a job, and more respect for property, you tend to be much less likely to commit crimes. For one, you've got less time to get into trouble. And two, you're working toward paying for your home, and it will take a long time. You don't want to spend all that time working toward this goal only to throw it away on a silly crime.

⊛  ⊛  ⊛

With all these benefits, it easy to see why governments like home ownership.

While these are all strong arguments, some of them are broadly applied, even though they really aren't broadly applicable. For instance, the health benefit of housing (not necessarily home ownership) is most applicable to the homeless and low-income populations. Providing housing to a homeless person in the form of subsidized housing obviously improves their situation, but it's not necessary to provide them with a house they own. Providing affordable housing to low-income populations prevents them from becoming homeless. Ownership is not required for the population to benefit from access to housing. It's less relevant to compare a middle-class homeowner to a middle-class renter. Whether owning or renting, both would clearly have a warm, safe place to sleep.

> Ownership is not required for the population to benefit from access to housing. Whether owning or renting, both provide a warm, safe place to sleep.

In fact, most of the population can afford to arrange (by buying or renting) clean and safe housing. The kind of housing that is beneficial to health is within reach of the vast majority of the population. When governments pursue pro–home ownership housing policy on the basis that a clean and safe residence is good for one's health, they are stretching the truth.

Other studies suggest that, even among those who can afford home ownership, homeowners are in better health than non-homeowners. However, the fact that homeowners have higher levels of health than non-homeowners doesn't necessarily mean that home ownership is making their health better. That would be like saying that because American's have a longer life expectancy than most nations and most American speak English, speaking English must make people live longer. Clearly this would be a wrong conclusion. Longer life expectancy among Americans is probably related more to having a safe, law-abiding society; advanced medical care; clean water and food supplies; and high levels of education (also proven to be associated with better health and longer lives).

The arguments used by governments to promote home ownership include the advertised reasons that governments and politicians use to justify pro–home ownership government policies. But the real reasons politicians support driving home ownership rates higher are more basic — and self-serving.

The pragmatic goal of almost any politician is to get elected and, once elected, to stay elected. After all, a politician who's not elected is just an unemployed politician. This is the case among all politicians, because for a genuine, benevolent politician who is there to serve the people, the only way to work to improve government is to be in power.

So how does promoting home ownership fit into the objective of getting and staying elected? Well, it is one of the only true Win/Win/Win issues.

Any policy that can help increase home ownership rates is popular with voters. It's popular because it means more voters will have achieved the Canadian or American or Australian or Croatian or Russian Dream of home ownership. That means more people feeling the pride of ownership.

To feel that pride of ownership, think about the first big thing you bought in your life that you had to save up for. It could have been a bicycle, a collector's-edition comic book, a mobile phone, a little black dress, or a car. It might have even been a home. Whatever it was, this thing was different from the moment you first got it.

> The pragmatic goal of almost any politician is to get and stay elected. Pro–home ownership policies fit into that objective.

Sure, you'd had things before, and maybe even an older, less shiny version of the same item. But this one was yours, and you'd worked hard to save to buy it. You liked looking at it, playing with it, and generally having it.

That's pride of ownership, and that great feeling makes voters happy. That's Win #1: Giving voters pride of ownership.

Win #2 is jobs. If more people can buy houses, more people will be needed to make houses. And appliances, furniture, paint, shingles, lumber, and lawnmowers. More people having jobs means more happy, productive people. This is part of the economic benefit of pro–home ownership policies.

Of course, Win #3 is for the politician, who wins because more voters are happily owning a home and happily holding down a job. When people own homes and have jobs, they are much more likely to vote for the politician who helped them get a home and a job.

Win/Win/Win! That's why politicians love policies that promote home ownership.

We don't even have to think back too long to come up with a recent example. Just before the October 2015 federal election, the Conservatives, led by a then quite unpopular Stephen Harper, reached for the Win/Win/Win home ownership strategy with a pledge to drive home ownership from about 70 percent up to 72.5 percent.

However, like all good things, home ownership is best in moderation. Only those people who are well suited for home ownership should become homeowners. The same goes for pro–home ownership policies. There's a point where you can have too much pro–home ownership policy.

The challenge with these policies is that the benefits of increasing home ownership are generally one-time benefits. The home ownership rate can only increase from 65 to 66 percent once. To get more benefit, the next policy needs to increase the home ownership rate from 66 to 67 percent. So, once a policy to increase home ownership is put in place, the problem becomes that it can never be taken away without having the equal and opposite impact on home ownership. Removing those policies can reduce home ownership rates, have a negative impact on employment, and have a generally depressing effect on voter sentiment. That kind of negative impact is Lose/Lose/Lose for politicians.

There have been many articles, reports, papers, and discussions over the past few years about the role U.S. pro–home ownership policies might have played in the recent and sustained crash in U.S. house prices following 2006. I think it's fair to say that a good example of taking housing policy too far is the American Dream Downpayment Initiative, which George Bush announced when he made the speech in 2002 that I mentioned earlier. That fund was created to give grants of money, to be used as down payments, to people who couldn't save up a down payment themselves.

If you ask me, I think part of the societal benefit of home ownership gets eroded if you make it too easy to attain. Nevertheless, whether it's through mortgage insurance, interest deductibility, zoning policies, rental market restrictions, or other forms of pro–home ownership policy, governments and politicians are keen to see more homeowners for the benefit of the country … and the benefit of their re-election prospects.

# CHAPTER 16
## What Have the Rule Makers Been Up To?

It is true that the Canadian government wants Canadians to be homeowners, and it's true that huge amounts of time and money are spent on managing Canada's housing market. Managing it has gotten more complicated and challenging over the past couple of decades as interest rates have fallen, the U.S. housing market has collapsed, and a huge amount of attention and scrutiny has been paid to the Canadian housing market. The Canadian government has been active on housing policy recently, and it has made some changes that have already likely affected Canadian house prices and will continue to do so.

By 2004, Canada was looking a little behind the times when it came to pro–home ownership housing policy relative to the United States. The U.S. mortgage industry had been innovating aggressively under the encouragement of George W. Bush, creating innovative financial products that packaged up mortgages into bonds called residential mortgage-backed securities and fostering a new sub-prime mortgage market for aspiring homeowners with bad credit ratings.

The terms of these mortgages got ever more aggressive, with minimum down payments disappearing, credit checks becoming optional, and even cash-back arrangements available, in which the mortgage would pay for the whole house and then provide more money so new homebuyers could furnish their new homes with new furniture. Some mortgages had adjustable rates that started out for a fixed period at an unreasonably low interest rate as a way to encourage more buyers to enter the housing market.

Not to be outdone, CMHC began following the lead of the U.S. market in the early 2000s, with more innovative and flexible mortgage terms like 2004's Flex Down program, which allowed prospective homebuyers to borrow the required 5-percent down payment, where previously homebuyers had to attest that the down payment was part of their savings or a gift from a close relative.

In 2005, CMHC began offering mortgage insurance for a homeowner's second year-round home. By 2006, CMHC formally eliminated the requirement for any down payment, with the Flex 100 program (as in, the mortgage covered 100 percent of the purchase price). During 2006 alone, CMHC extended the maximum amortization period from twenty-five years to thirty years, then to thirty-five years, and finally out to forty years. In March 2007, the minimum down payment to avoid the requirement for mortgage insurance was reduced by the federal government from 25 to 20 percent.

All of these moves were taken to support CMHC's mission, which is to "Promote housing quality, affordability, and choice for Canadians." I'd also argue that these moves were taken to encourage more home ownership and the economic activity that home ownership generates for the Canadian economy.

Looking back, it seems pretty clear Canada was headed in the same direction as the United States was, only we were a little late to the party. Fortunately, the risks of relaxing all of these rules and regulations were made clear by the collapse of the U.S. housing market beginning in 2007.

In short order, CMHC began to roll back the changes it had implemented over the previous few years, with the maximum amortization period cut from forty years to thirty-five years in October 2008 and the minimum down payment restored to 5 percent of the purchase price, up from zero.

As the full extent of the damage of the housing collapse in the United States became clear over the following few years, mortgage insurance rules continued to be tightened, with limits on the leverage available on refinancing reduced in 2010, 2011, and 2012. In 2011, the maximum amortization was reduced to thirty years from thirty-five years, and then again in 2012 it was restored to its original twenty-five-year term.

Further tightening of regulations came in 2014 and 2015, including the elimination of mortgage insurance for homes priced above $1 million, higher mortgage insurance premiums, and higher minimum down payment requirements for more expensive homes.

All of these recent changes are highly unusual in that they are not pro–home ownership and they don't make it easier and cheaper for Canadians to buy homes. Quite the opposite. Canada has seen more than a dozen changes to individual mortgage-lending rules, all of which make it more difficult and expensive to buy housing. Apparently, watching the largest residential housing crash of modern times take place next door gave our government the courage to resist the temptation of pro–home ownership policies and take action to protect the Canadian housing market.

> Since the start of the U.S. housing crisis, Canada has seen more than a dozen changes to mortgage-lending rules, all of which make it more difficult and expensive to buy housing.

With continued speculation about whether Canada's housing market is currently in a bubble, it's interesting to note that the most powerful regulator of mortgage financing in Canada has taken several steps, over several years, to reduce risks to the Canadian housing market. Behind almost every major financial or asset market collapse in modern financial history is a regulator that loosened regulations or failed to keep up with newly evolving businesses.

With rapid price appreciation in home prices in the Vancouver and Toronto markets in 2016, there could be further actions taken to cool demand for home ownership in attempts to slow the growth in home prices.

Whatever the future holds for Canadian house prices, it seems our regulators have been acting in a conservative and responsible manner. CMHC looks like it's been doing a heck of a job!

# CHAPTER 17

## How Housing Can Dictate Your Career in Surprising and Unexpected Ways

We've been looking a lot into the various financial and non-financial reasons offered by those who think it's a good idea for you to buy a home. I'd like to focus now on the impact that your choice in housing can have on your career. As we'll see, for many, renting, which is usually the cheapest housing option available, can allow a worker more employment options.

If you're like most people, the two things you'll spend most of your life doing are sleeping and working. If you sleep eight hours a night, you're racking up close to 3 thousand hours a year in the sack. A little more when you're a teenager, a little less once you're an adult, and even less when you have infant twins.

Because we spend so much time sleeping, and because how well we sleep determines how well we feel while we're awake, I've always made sleeping well a priority. A good night's sleep is best had on a comfortable mattress.

So I'm a big believer in investing in a good mattress. There's nothing quite like a brand-new, perfect mattress. At the mattress store they'll tell you a mattress is good for about a thousand nights and that we should replace our mattress every few years. I don't know if there's any science behind that, and we need to be careful taking advice about a purchase from the people trying to sell us the product. (Remember, everyone else wins when you buy a house.) But it seems to me that most people I talk to haven't bought a new mattress in many years. I think that's a shame. Mattresses have gotten a whole lot better over time, and the newest ones are truly delightful. Maybe every other year is too often, but if you've been sleeping on the same mattress for more than five years, I think you should make a note to yourself to take a trip to the mattress store and see what you've been missing. Sure, it will cost you a good chunk of money, but if you sleep better, you'll enjoy life more, and that includes work. Which is the thing we spend the second most time in our lives doing.

Because we'll spend close to two thousand hours a year for most of our working lives doing whatever it is that we do to make money, I think we should make sure that we have the best "mattress" — job — we can find.

Your high school guidance counsellor wouldn't be doing a good job if he or she didn't tell you to do what you love. Maybe you heard that last week, or maybe it's been a few years (or more) since you last sat down with a guidance counsellor. Either way, I think that advice is very, very good. (Notice that they aren't trying to sell you anything?) So why do so many people work at jobs that fail to inspire them, or worse? After all, it's the thing we spend most of our time doing other than sleeping.

For most of us, one really big reason we work at jobs we don't love is money. But money's not enough for everyone. We all know someone who's doing something they love. Maybe it's a friend from high school who is following his dream of becoming a rock star, working odd jobs to eke by. Or another friend who taught English in Korea, travelled the world, and took some courses at the local college while she lived in her parents' basement before starting a dog walking service (which actually pays pretty well, from what I hear).

While our friends are loving what they do, they most likely aren't carrying a large mortgage that will take twenty-five years to pay back. That's not a coincidence. In Canada, if you want to own a home, you need a good-paying job that gives you a steady and reliable income. That means homeowners generally can't afford to be unemployed for long, choose jobs that don't pay enough to support the costs of ownership, or choose jobs that might be unreliable.

Of course, some of us are lucky enough to not only love what we do, but also get paid well to do it. But even in those lucky cases, the effect of a mortgage on your working life can be dramatic.

Every job, no matter how good, will have some weaknesses. An arrogant boss. The co-worker who never gets their work done on time, forcing everyone else to pick up the slack. Silly corporate policies. At one point in my career, the company I worked for gave me a company credit card with a

$20,000 limit, yet at the same time I wasn't able to use the colour printer without first getting explicit approval from my boss. Every single time.

Industries change, companies change, and jobs change. What might be a dream job today could head downhill for many reasons. If you find yourself in a bad job, you'll likely want to change jobs. It could be to another company doing the same thing. It might be to a whole new career in a different job in a different industry.

If and when you find yourself in that situation, the decisions you've made about housing will have a very significant impact on what options you have.

Banks will tell you that you can afford a house for which the mortgage payments, property taxes, and utilities equal 32 percent of your income. That seems like a pretty reasonable thing. After your housing costs, what's left should cover all the other expenses of a reasonable lifestyle — food, clothes, entertainment, and everything else that we normally do with our money.

> The simple fact that you're locked in with a house purchase, that you've lost the option to leave, can affect how much you enjoy your job.

But the most important word in that sentence is *can*. You *can* afford a house that costs you 32 percent of your income. But you certainty don't *have to* buy a house that costs you 32 percent of your income.

If you do buy a house that costs you 32 percent of your income, you can really only take jobs that pay the same amount as the job you want to leave. Otherwise, you won't be able to afford the house and all the other things in life you were spending your money on. And you never know. It might be worse than a bad job. Your job could be downsized, the industry you work in could fall on bad times, or the company could go out of business. Even governments go through periods of budget cuts and layoffs.

To take it a little further, for anyone with the slightest bit of commitment-phobia, buying a house is a big commitment — both in terms of a commitment to a mortgage you'll have to pay for a long time and a commitment to continue to make as much or more than you're making for a long time. That simple fact, that you're locked in, that you have lost the option to leave, can affect how much you enjoy your job.

Warren Buffett, one of the world's greatest investors, once said that he has a practice of hiring CEOs who are already wealthy to run the companies he owns. That way he knows they are taking the job because they want the job, not because they need the job. That means that they'll be happy, productive, and engaged. What I take away from that message is that the day you know you can walk away from your job at any minute is the day that you look at work through a whole new lens. It fundamentally changes the way that you work. It changes the way you'll act at work.

If you don't need your job, you won't have to consider whether your actions might put your job at risk. If a colleague suggests something you completely disagree with, you're going to say something about it. Because you aren't worried about losing your job. If you are freer to speak you mind and have good ideas, you're likely to be better at your job.

Most people won't be able to achieve the financial freedom that is required to be able to walk out on a good job that pays a decent wage, but you don't have to reach that extreme to have job-dependence change how well you like your job and how well you do at your job. Job dependence is a continuum, and the more you need your job, the more limited you've made your work options. Even moving down the job dependence scale can significantly improve your job flexibility and enjoyment.

Consider three different situations. Three professionals, all are in their mid-thirties, and all are single. All three work in the same job at a company, each makes $60,000 per year, and all three have become unhappy with their work.

The first of the three is José, who has been working at the Wet Banana Flooring Company for six years. José thinks that Wet Banana is a great company but that their main product, laminate flooring, is too slippery. He thinks that the company is missing out on a lot more sales because they haven't figured out how to make their flooring less slippery.

José has been renting for the last ten years. While he's been renting, he's been responsible and saved up a little money each month for the last ten years and now has $75,000 in savings. He's renting a nice, relatively small apartment (he's just one guy), and he pays $1,000 per month.

The second Wet Banana employee is Tami. She's been with the company for eight years, and she also thinks the company is missing out on a huge opportunity by not improving the traction of their flooring. Tami bought a small but comfortable townhouse five years ago. She put down $30,000 as a down payment on her $240,000 house. Since then, Tami's house has risen in value to $260,000 and she's paid down another $10,000 off of her mortgage, paying a little extra here and there to speed up the repayment. Tami pays $900 toward her mortgage and another $200 in property taxes each month.

Finally, we have George. He's been at Wet Banana for seven years, and George also thinks the company could do a lot better with a few minor changes to their flooring products. George bought his dream home ten years ago. It's a gorgeous four-bedroom house in a nice neighbourhood, and he loves it. He paid $400,000 for it and made a down payment of $20,000. Since then, his house has risen in value to $460,000, and he's paid down $15,000. He continues to pay $1,800 per month to the mortgage and pays another $300 in property taxes.

José, Tami, and George all work for Stu. Stu's father, Ken, founded Wet Banana Flooring forty years ago and retired a few years previous, leaving Stu in charge of the company. Except Stu doesn't know the flooring industry as well as his dad does, and he hasn't been making the right decisions. Stu also has a reputation of always wanting to be right and getting pretty angry when he's made to look foolish.

Now, given that we have three similar people working for the same company, in the same job, how might the different housing decisions they've made affect how they are likely to address the company's problems?

George knows Stu well — well enough to know that changing his mind about his slippery flooring products won't be easy. But George also knows that if he can change Stu's mind, the company will do much better and that will be good for everyone, including George, particularly if Stu recognizes that George helped him turn things around.

Yet George wants to be extremely careful about how he tries to convince Stu that things need to change. Mainly because he knows that he's got a great salary at Wet Banana, and that if he had to find another job, the only other flooring company in town, Flat Tiles, pays its employees about 10 percent less than Wet Banana. With his mortgage payments, he can't afford to lose his job. Even if he managed to get a job at Flat Tiles, it wouldn't be enough to cover his mortgage. He's already stretched. If he were to lose his job, he'd be in trouble. He's got close to $100,000 of equity in his home, which is the good news, but the bad news is that the monthly cost of living in his house is high. If he were forced to sell, the transaction costs on a sale would be almost $25,000, wiping out a quarter of the equity in his home.

So George decides that he'd rather not risk the good thing he's got going. After all, he's got a great house and a good income, and the only thing he needs to do is keep doing a good job, not upset his temperamental boss Stu, and take comfort in the fact that there's enough money in slippery tiles to keep Wet Banana in business.

Then comes Tami. She's been thinking the same things as George has for a while now and is debating what do. She knows Stu doesn't often take advice well, but she thinks there's a good chance that she'll be able to convince Stu that she's right and that they should change their flooring.

Tami needs her job. She's got a mortgage, and she couldn't last too long without an income before she ran into trouble with her mortgage. But because Tami was more modest with her house purchase, she knows that if worst comes to worst, she can probably get a job with Flat Tiles. Even though they pay a little less than Wet Banana, Tami can get by on less income. So Tami gets prepared to pull Stu aside and have a chat about the ideas she has about new, less slippery tiles.

At the same time, José, who also sees a lot of things that could be done better at Wet Banana, has been having the same thoughts. He knows Stu is hard-headed and that it's tough to change his mind. And he knows that confronting Stu with a whole bunch of ideas about how Wet Banana Flooring Comany could really turn things around might prompt Stu to fire him.

But José is in a very different spot than Tami or George. He's got modest housing costs of just $1,000 a month and he's saved a $75,000 nest egg that he can fall back on if he finds himself out of a job. Because he's been renting, he could, if he needed to, find a new, cheaper place to live without paying huge transaction costs. In fact, he can probably get by quite comfortably for a few years without any income, in a worst-case scenario.

You can see where this is going. José can afford to lose his job and can easily get by if he takes a job at Flat Tiles or even a lower-paying job in another industry, if he has to. He's in a great position to take the risk of upsetting Stu to improve Wet Banana's business and do what he thinks is the right thing to do.

Tami is likely going to take a softer approach to pushing Stu to make some changes. She might be successful or she might not, but she's definitely not going to risk her job to help the company out. George is out of luck. He's taken on too much risk with his housing decision and, as a result, doesn't want to even bring up his ideas with Stu because he absolutely can't afford to lose his job.

This example is about whether each of the employees has the freedom and flexibility to speak their minds, but it's more than that. Only José can do what he believes is right for the company, and do so with all of his abilities. José is a better employee, and more valuable to Wet Banana, than either Tami or George. José has also set himself up better to succeed in his career, maintaining the flexibility to do what he thinks is right and take the risks that could ultimately give him the edge over Tami and George when it comes time for promotions and raises.

Of course, Stu might not agree with José's ideas if he isn't diplomatic about voicing his concerns, and may ultimately decide to fire José. But it's been a long time since employees stayed with one company their entire lives, and while being more financially flexible might encourage you to be more vocal or aggressive in promoting your ideas and your career, burdening yourself with too much financial commitment almost certainly will have a negative impact on your ability to do the right thing for your company and advance your career. It will limit your ability to pursue other work opportunities that might not be as financially rewarding but could offer better career advancement or more exciting and rewarding work.

> Burdening yourself with too much financial commitment almost certainly will have a negative impact on your ability to do the right thing for your company and advance your career.

The effect of having a mortgage on behaviour at work and career progression is probably the furthest thing from a first-time homebuyer's mind when they're in the heat of one of Canada's high-pressure bidding wars. Yet, for the thing we spend the second-largest portion of our lives doing, our housing decisions can hold us back or propel us forward in our careers. And on this point, there is no contest. Renting is much better for your career than owning.

# CHAPTER 18

## Forced Savings:
## The Secret of the Wealthy Renter

If the numbers don't lie and housing has consistently delivered mediocre returns over the long term, how come housing so consistently appears as the largest, most valuable asset most households own? Why do people consistently choose this investment over all the others that would provide better returns?

The stock market seems riskier and more volatile. Bonds seem like they'll never make you any money (especially in a low interest-rate environment). Commodities are scary. And you can't live in any of these other investments. Those factors might be part of the answer, but there's a bigger reason: forced savings.

Forced savings is the term used to describe mandatory payments that create savings for the person making them.

The truth is that buying a house is a simple and structured forced-savings plan. Many people identify with the concept that if you rent for your entire life, you'll have been paying rent for a lifetime and you'll be left with nothing.

That could be true, but it doesn't have to be.

It's true if you compare two very similar people with the same jobs, incomes, and families, both of whom spend whatever income is left over on consumption items. If one of them rents and one of them has bought their home, the one who bought their home will have been forced to save some of their income solely because of the fact that they will have had to make mortgage payments (some of which will have gone toward the payment of the principal on their mortgage).

Let's consider the following case. A renter is paying $1,200 a month, plus about $100 per month in utilities. An owner bought a house for $250,000 and is paying about $1,300 a month in mortgage payments. But the owner is also paying $200 a month in property taxes, plus $100 for utilities. And then there's the maintenance, which only happens every so often (replacing a fridge, the roof, the driveway, or other items) but over the long run probably costs at least $425 per month. (The rule of thumb for mainten-

> The secret
> to renting is in
> what is done with
> the difference between
> what a homeowner
> spends on housing
> and what a renter
> spends.

ance costs is 2 to 5 percent of the value of the house in most markets, and lower where house prices are particularly high.) So the owner is paying about $1,950 per month for housing, while the renter is paying $1,300.

Assuming that's the end of the story, at the end of a twenty-five-year mortgage and twenty-five years of renting, the homeowner would have a $320,600 home (assuming a 1-percent increase in price each year), completely free and clear, while the renter would have nothing.

That's the math most people do when they look at this argument.

It's on this basis that many, many people get comfortable with the idea of buying a house. They know that if they commit to paying off their mortgage over a long time, they'll find themselves, at the other end, owning their home, which should provide a very comfortable base for a nice retirement.

But the secret to renting is in what is done with the other $650 per month. What "other" $650 per month? That's the difference between what the homeowner is spending on housing and what the renter is spending.

The renter can do any number of different things with his or her extra $650 per month. Vacations, lottery tickets, home entertainment, nights out on the town with friends, nice cars, presents for family and friends at the holidays, or retirement savings.

If you're like 95 percent of people, odds are that at least one of the items listed would appeal more than "retirement savings." That's just natural. Saving for retirement doesn't sound sexy. It doesn't sound like fun. It sounds more like a punishment than a luxury.

But that's really what buying a home will provide you with, a long, long way down the road, once you've paid off the mortgage. A portion, which increases over time, of the $1,300 mortgage payment goes to paying down the mortgage. While these numbers are a fictional generalization, they are similar to the proportions that many renters and owners pay relative to each other.

So back to the $650. That's $7,800 per year, or $195,000 over the course of twenty-five years. That $195,000 would be what a renter would have if they were to stuff $650 per month under her mattress. If, instead, the renter had deposited $650 per month into the S&P/TSX Composite Index starting in 1991 and ending in 2015, that $195,000 of monthly deposits would have grown to $660,000 over twenty-five years.

That's a huge number! But it's only a number that can be real if a renter actually saves the other $650. That can take an awful lot of discipline.

We're all guilty of giving in to our impulsiveness and desire for nice things. We have ingrained social behaviours that encourage consumption and the accumulation of material goods. It's easy to get accustomed to enjoying a laid-back, indulgent lifestyle. But that kind of behaviour usually doesn't work out too well in the long run.

For many Canadians, this forced payment into a mortgage is the only contribution to savings they will consistently make. For this reason alone, it is a good thing that many financially undisciplined Canadians believe in "Why Rent When You Can Buy?" Otherwise, they may never accumulate any other substantial financial assets.

Perhaps most notably, for homes bought twenty-five years ago, regular principal amortization payments account for between 25 and 40 percent of the ending value of the home, depending on what city you live in. By comparison, in the earlier example of a renter investing in the TSX, the principal contributions to savings accounted for 30 percent of the ending value. So, in many cases, those who invest in the stock market will have to contribute less of their income to achieve the same savings as is necessary for those who invest in home ownership. In both cases, though, whether one invests in a home or in the stock market,

The forced savings element of mortgage payments is a function of the financing structure, and is available from a number of other savings programs.

the discipline of making regular payments into a savings program is clearly critical to building wealth.

It is important to recognize that the discipline associated with home ownership is not a result of the asset purchased (a home), but rather the financing structure used by most homebuyers. The forced savings element of mortgage payments is what gives home ownership the fabulous reputation it has as a cornerstone of so many Canadians' personal wealth not the performance of home prices.

Here's the fantastic news: That financing structure is available from a number of other savings programs. Even some that you likely already participate in.

The critical elements of a forced savings program are that there is a regular payment and there is an incentive or penalty in place to ensure the payment takes place. By adding the incentive or penalty, the payment takes on a higher priority in the saver's financial decisions. Some programs are truly forced, while others are more flexible, but the incentive or penalty needs to strongly encourage payments to be made.

Here are nine alternative options for setting up a forced savings program. If you don't want to own a home but want the financial security associated with home ownership, one of these might be just right for you.

## AUTOMATIC TRANSFERS

An automatic transfer is a payment anyone can set up though their bank, where money is transferred from one account to another. Automatic transfers can be set up between any kind of accounts. For instance, a transfer could be set up to move 10 percent of each paycheque to an RRSP account, a TSFA account, a taxable investment account, or even just a savings account. You can arrange for these transfers to occur every two weeks or every month, and once they are set up, you don't have to remember to do anything. They will automatically happen and, over time, the money will build up.

While the payment here is automatic, the trick to making this program work is ensuring there is enough money in the account each time a transfer occurs. By setting the transfer up on the same day a paycheque is deposited, you can maximize the odds of this program working well for you.

## PREMIUM TERM LIFE INSURANCE POLICIES

These life insurance policies combine a life insurance policy that pays a specific amount in the event that the insured person dies during the fixed term of the policy, with a savings plan, which, at the end of the term, returns the accumulated value of the policy at the end of the term to the policy holder. Think about this option like life insurance that pays out at a specified date, whether you die or not. These policies can make a lot of sense for people who have strong income prospects over a long period of time, significant dependents (children or otherwise), and high debt levels, such as doctors in the early years of their careers who might have student debt and be starting families.

## CORPORATE SHARE PURCHASE LOANS

I am fortunate enough to work for a company that offers one of these gems. The idea is that the company you work for will lend you money to buy shares of the company. Once the loan is made and the shares are purchased, the employee makes regular payments, often automatically deducted from their paycheque or withdrawn from their chequing account, to pay the interest on the loan and to pay down the loan, just like a mortgage. The only difference is that the asset that the loan is used to purchase is shares in a company, rather than a home.

Of course, this kind of program isn't available at every company, and government employees or people who work at companies without these plans are out of luck.

This kind of program has risks. The shares of the company you work for could go down over time or the company could go bankrupt. It can be a pretty concentrated investment compared to an investment spread across a number of different companies or different asset classes, such as stocks, bonds, and income-producing real estate. If you work in a highly cyclical industry, like commodities (energy and mining are big businesses in Canada), or a rapidly evolving industry, like technology, you probably don't want the majority of your savings tied up in one company. Conversely, shares in broadly diversified companies or regulated industries can be highly appealing. Either way, employee share loans do offer the discipline of a forced savings program.

## AUTOMATIC PAYROLL DEDUCTIONS

A lot of companies offer payroll deduction programs, where amounts are deducted from your paycheque before you even see it. In fact, pretty much every company has automatic payroll deductions, like the amounts for income taxes, employment insurance, or the Canada Pension Plan (or QPP for people in Quebec).

But a lot of companies offer additional programs in which employees can sign up to have a certain amount or percentage of their paycheques automatically sent somewhere else. Some employers offer programs in which the automatic deductions go to pay for things like health insurance, parking passes, or charity donations. Many also offer the option of having automatic payroll deductions directed into savings programs, like RRSPs, taxable investment accounts, bank savings accounts, or other programs. These programs are great because they happen before you see your money. Just like *The Wealthy Barber* says, paying yourself first is great because you forget about it, it just happens, and before you know it, the savings have grown into a significant nest egg.

## BOND PURCHASE PROGRAMS

The government of Canada, through the Bank of Canada, sells Canada Savings Bonds. These bonds offer a fixed interest rate for the first year the bond is owned, which is reset for the second year and the third (and final) year of the bond. These bonds are cashable (you can get your money back) at any time. There are also Canada Premium Bonds, which offer a higher interest rate but can be redeemed (sold) only during the month after which you purchased the bond each year.

These bonds can be purchased through a payroll deduction program the government has established. Hundreds of Canadian companies have joined this program (including mine), allowing for a regular automatic deduction from employee paycheques of contributions to this savings program.

The interest rates on these bonds are quite low, currently close to 1 percent per year, so they aren't going to generate high returns for investors. However, they are backed by the Government of Canada, and there is zero chance they will not deliver the stated return. These bonds are particularly well suited to the most risk-averse investors.

## DIVIDEND REINVESTMENT PROGRAMS

This one might be the easiest and most painless forced savings program of all. The dividend or distribution reinvestment program is often referred to as a DRIP. Many publicly traded companies that pay regular dividends or distributions (cash payments) to the owners of the stock in the company offer a dividend or distribution reinvestment program.

For investors who sign up for the DRIP program, instead of paying you cash dividends on a monthly or quarterly basis, the company will instead take the cash amount and issue the same value in new shares or units in the company. So over time, if you were to, for instance, buy 100 shares of a company offering a 5-percent dividend yield, a year later you might have 105 shares. Ten years later you might have something closer to 150 shares. On top of having more shares, the price of the shares might have gone up and the dividends might have increased.

When you retire and you are looking for more income to support your retirement years, you could cancel your dividend reinvestment plan and take the cash dividends. Because you participated in the plan, you would have dividends on 150 shares, for which you had to pay for only 100 out of pocket, to provide income. Pretty sweet, if you ask me!

In my day job, I analyze over forty Canadian REITs, nearly half of which offer a DRIP program. All of the Canadian banks also have one, and many other Canadian companies offer these programs. They're easy and painless ways to build wealth.

## CORPORATE MATCHING PROGRAMS

These programs come in all shapes and sizes, and they are all designed to encourage employees to save for retirement. The typical structure is that a percentage of the employee's contribution is matched by the company and can be focused on the purchase of shares of the company or, more broadly, on a contribution to a retirement savings program, like an RRSP.

Usually these programs will have a limit to how much an employee can contribute, and because of the limited dollar value, the percentage of contributions the company matches can be very high. It's not uncommon for a company to contribute 50 percent to a matching program in which an employee contributes up to a small percentage of their annual income (usually 3 to 5 percent) to a registered retirement savings program or a share purchase program. These programs are usually set up with an automatic payroll deduction plan, as described earlier, but are also offered where an employee can contribute once a year.

These programs are designed to encourage employees to save for the future. With a 50-percent contribution from the company, even if the investment doesn't rise in value, you're getting a great return. These programs are quite popular, with a lot of people describing them as "free money." If you don't know if your employer offers one of these programs, it's worth investigating. There aren't many places you can find free money!

## GOVERNMENT RETIREMENT PROGRAMS

The ultimate in forced savings, a government-administered retirement plan, like the Canada Pension Plan (CPP), leaves you no option but to save for the future. Unless you get paid cash, "under the table," or less than $3,500 per year, you have to contribute to the CPP. If you are working for a company, those contributions are made automatically, before you ever have a chance to spend the money on anything else.

The Canada Pension Plan has over $270 billion dollars of retirement savings that it manages on behalf of over 18 million Canadians. Employers must make mandatory contributions in the amount of 4.95 percent of employee wages from the employee and another 4.95 percent from the employer, totalling 9.9 percent of employee wages. If you live in Quebec, you don't participate in the CPP but instead have to participate in the Quebec Pension Plan, which is similar to the CPP.

The maximum amount of benefit in 2016 from the CPP is $1,092.50 per month. That's $13,110 per year. Fortunately, if you hit the maximum CPP payment, you might also be eligible for another one of Canada's federal retirement programs, Old Age Security (OAS). The maximum amount available under the OAS program, depending on your marital status and income, is $1,213 per month. OAS is different from a lot of retirement savings programs in that it doesn't require any contributions, but it is generally available to all Canadians over the age of sixty-five who have lived in Canada for the last ten years, with a few loopholes and exceptions.

## EMPLOYER PENSIONS

A lot of companies provide employees with a mandatory pension plan, particularly large companies. According to Statistics Canada, 38 percent of all employees in Canada have an employer pension plan. Employer pensions usually don't involve contributions from the employee, but rather contributions are made by the employer, typically based on the employee's income level. There are two primary types of pension plans: defined benefit, which pays a fixed benefit amount upon retirement, and defined contribution, in which the benefit payments in the future depend on the performance of the investment held by the pension. The contributions made into a defined contribution pension fund are fixed.

## PLAIN OLD-FASHIONED DISCIPLINE

This is probably the least successful investing program of all time. Unless you are obsessively focused on building wealth, there are always more interesting and immediately satisfying things you can do with your money. Whether you're into travel or cars, home entertainment, clothes, collectibles, pedicures, or any number of other things we can all spend money on, voluntarily taking a chunk of every paycheque and directing it toward your savings account is challenging. Some people have that drive to save, and for them this is really a forced savings program. But for everyone else, this is like a New Year's resolution: It is a great idea, and everyone agrees with that. Then life happens, and it gets lost in the things that require immediate attention and action.

This is the worst savings program of all, mainly because it very rarely works. Piggy banks are more successful.

## CONCLUSION

With the forced savings program embedded in mortgages the real driver of housing-based wealth, and the ability of renters to set up a similar forced savings program through many other programs, many of which have provided better returns than home prices have, renters can have their cake and eat it too. None of the commitment, responsibility, financial risk, or high transaction costs of home ownership, but all of the wealth creation benefits of a forced savings program. Setting up a forced savings program is a critical element of renting the Wealthy Renter way!

# CHAPTER 19

## Retirement and Housing

Most people hope to retire someday. Retirement promises different benefits for each person. For some people, it means golf six days a week, winters in Florida (or Arizona, or somewhere else warm), and spending more time pursuing hobbies. For others, it means having more time to volunteer for local organizations, travel to far-off places, and spend time with friends and family. Some see retirement as offering the opportunity to give up a lucrative but unsatisfying job for something more satisfying at lower pay, on a part-time basis, or even on a volunteer basis.

However you might imagine your retirement, what most have in common is the lack of a full-time, wage-paying job. That usually means a decline in income, compared to what the retiree was making before retirement. To make ends meet, retirees typically need to either reduce expenses or increase their income.

Paying off a mortgage can reduce monthly expenses, making it seem like an ideal target for homeowners just ahead of retirement. Homeowners know that if they get desperate and need money, they can sell their home. So, naturally, many homeowners look at housing as something of a retirement fund.

There's a compelling logic to the idea, and of course a house, unlike other kinds of investments, also provides a home to live in. You might have even heard someone say, "You can't live in a stock portfolio." There is certainly truth to that statement. But there are also problems with relying on a home as a retirement fund.

In Chapter 4 we talked about the concept of "over-consuming" housing. That's when a homeowner is spending more of their income on their housing than they think they are and, as a result, ends up having a whole lot less to spend on all the other things in life. Anyone can over-consume housing, including renters, but over-consuming housing is a particularly high risk for retiree homeowners, including the baby boomers who have begun to retire recently. Housing needs change significantly over the course of our lives, but a confluence of factors conspire to keep retirees in homes too large and too expensive for their needs. The inconvenience, disruption, and high cost of moving; personal ties to the community; and the general inertia of owning mean that many homeowners stay in housing that no longer meets their needs as they retire. Empty nesters, for instance, often stay in the same homes they raised their children in, despite having significantly more space than they need, after their children move out.

The math most homeowners run when figuring out their housing costs encourages the over-consumption of housing.

> Whether you're a homeowner without a mortgage, a homeowner with a mortgage, or a renter, the cost of living in a home is the same.

Every situation is different, but it's not uncommon to see the monthly expenses relating to a house drop by half or more once a mortgage is paid off, which is a lot. So there is a big reduction in costs once a homeowner pays off their mortgage. Or is there?

We have to remember that, whether you're a homeowner without a mortgage, a homeowner with a mortgage, or a renter, the cost of living in a home is the same. All that is different is who we pay the rent to: the landlord, the bank, or ourselves. In addition to the regular costs of housing a homeowner without a mortgage faces, like property taxes, utilities, and maintenance, there's also the opportunity cost or implicit rent. Implicit rent is particularly interesting when it comes to retirement.

While paying off a mortgage reduces the cash expenses, the total cost of living in a home, including implicit rent, doesn't change whether you rent, own with a mortgage, or own without a mortgage. That can be a problem for a retiree homeowner who is trying to reduce their expenses.

The problem is twofold. First, it's very easy for a homeowner to be unaware of how much implicit rent they are paying, particularly as they retire their mortgage. Second, it is extremely difficult to reduce the cost of home ownership without selling the home.

The implicit rent homeowners pay themselves is a real number, and it's a number that retiree homeowners should know. Until a retiree knows how much they're spending on housing, they can't decide whether they want to continue to spend that much on housing or find new housing that is less expensive and maybe more in line with their needs. The savings of right-sized housing could be used for all sorts of things, like travel and experiences, hobbies, gifts for loved ones, charitable donations, and even estate planning.

> Owning a home going into retirement can put you in the awkward position of either over-consuming housing or facing the significant cost of selling a home.

Renters always know exactly how much they are paying for housing. If it's too much, they'll notice, and because it's inexpensive for renters to move, they often move to housing that fits their needs. Homeowners, however, will find it much harder to reduce the cost of living in a home. Taking on room-mates is an option, but that is an uncomfortable prospect for many retirees. Other than sharing the cost of the home with someone else, the only way to reduce the cost of ownership in a significant way is to sell the home. Owning a home going into retirement can put you in the awkward position of either over-consuming housing or facing the significant cost of selling a home.

Let's consider a couple, Val and Zain, who live in Toronto today. They own a home in Toronto that they bought for $350,000 in 1996 with a $35,000 down payment and a $315,000 mortgage. At the time, they had two young children and they had household income of $75,000 per year. With mortgage rates at 7 percent then, their mortgage payment was $2,225 per month. That worked out to about 36 percent of their pre-tax income.

When they bought it, the home was a bit of a stretch. Adding in property taxes, maintenance, and utilities, the percentage of their pre-tax income spent on housing was 48 percent, significantly higher than the 32-percent maximum recommended by CMHC. They were spending almost $3,300 a month on housing and just $2,100 on everything else in life.

Fortunately, their timing was excellent. House prices had fallen sharply in the early 1990s, and the average Toronto house price was just 2.9 times average household income. Over the next twenty years, mortgage rates fell to under 3 percent, and less than a decade after they bought, the greenbelt around Toronto was created. House prices more than tripled over the twenty years they've been homeowners in Toronto.

Fast forward to today. Val and Zain are empty nesters and their mortgage is almost paid off, a few years ahead of schedule. The couple is planning to retire once they make their last mortgage payment, which is now $1,500 per month with today's lower interest rates. With some raises along the way, their household income has grown to $125,000, leaving them with almost $7,800 per month in after-tax income. Of this, they are spending $4,250 on their housing, including the $1,500 mortgage payment, property taxes, maintenance, and utilities.

Retirement is looking good, with pension income of $60,000 per year. Val and Zain have made some tough sacrifices along the way, sharing one car and using public transit, and limiting vacations and other indulgences. But it has paid off, since they are now millionaires with an almost mortgage-free home worth $1.1 million dollars.

When they make their last mortgage payment and retire, they will see their monthly after-tax income drop from $7,800 to about $5,400, but with the mortgage paid off, their expenses will drop by $1,500. Overall, the couple will have income after the cost of housing of $2,600 per month, which is enough for them to maintain their current lifestyle and even take a vacation each year. But it's a long way from the glamorous lifestyle imagined when you say the word *millionaires*.

I think there a lot of Torontonians and Canadians living like Val and Zain, and they may not be aware how much they are spending on housing, and on housing they don't need.

Now let's see what this couple is missing out on by over-consuming housing. Spending nearly $2,800 of their $5,400 monthly after-tax income is high, but not crazy for a retired couple in Toronto who own a home without a mortgage. Adding in the implicit rent they are paying themselves shows how much their home is really costing them.

We'll use the S&P/TSX Dividend Aristocrats Index as our alternative investment, which is currently yielding 4 percent. Selling their house for

$1.10 million would leave Val and Zain with $1.05 million after brokerage fees, which could generate dividend income of $42,000 per year, or $3,500 per month. With attractive tax rates on dividends, selling their home and investing in dividend-paying stocks would raise the couple's monthly income to nearly $10,000 per month, and their after-tax income would rise to $8,750 per month.

Of course, they will still need to rent a place to live. Since they need less space than they had, renting a nice apartment in Toronto could reasonably cost $2,500 per month. Selling their home to rent a smaller apartment that better meets their needs would reduce their housing costs and increase their income significantly. All told, Val and Zain's after-tax income, after the cost of housing, would rise from the $2,600 per month they would be getting if they still owned the home up to $6,250 per month!

The more than doubling of their income after taxes and housing costs opens up all sorts of opportunities for the couple, like exotic vacations, a new car, entertainment and restaurants, or any other thing they would like to spend their extra $3,650 per month on. That's an astounding $43,800 of extra cash income per year that they can spend without digging in to savings!

What about the risks of investing in the stock market? What if the market crashed? The beauty of the Dividend Aristocrats Index is that it is broadly diversified, with seventy-eight different stocks in the portfolio, and each one is selected based on its track record of regularly increasing dividends over time. Which brings us to the other significant risk of relying on a home as a retirement fund: having all your eggs in one basket, as they say. The riskiest part of relying on a home as a retirement fund is the concentration of all of your wealth in a single, high-value asset. In the investment industry, diversification is a critical tool for managing and reducing risk. Owning assets across a number of different investments can improve returns and reduce risks. You will never find a financial advisor who recommends putting all of your savings in a single investment. That is because all investments, including homes, involve some risk.

> The riskiest part of relying on a home as a retirement fund is the concentration of all of your wealth in a single, high-value asset.

That might sound a bit scary, and it should. It doesn't matter what you invest in, how much you know about that investment, or how confident you might be, it's impossible to predict the future with 100-percent certainty. The value of investments changes as conditions change. Changes in governments, technological innovation and disruption, natural disasters, demographic shifts, epidemics, monetary policy changes, corruption and scandals, currency fluctuations, shifts in trade policies, changes in tax rates, and any unending number of other factors can affect the price of investments, including homes.

To protect against the unknown future, professional investors spread their investments across a number of different assets. That means spreading your investments across a variety of asset types, including bonds, stocks, shopping malls, power plants, and other instruments. While they expect all of the investments to provide attractive returns, by having a number of different investments they reduce the risk of a surprise that heavily affects one of their investments from having such a large impact on their overall portfolio.

While diversification is one of the most basic tenets of professional investing, when it comes to homes, millions of Canadians concentrate their retirement savings into a single investment. House prices in Canada haven't seen a sustained decline across most markets in over twenty years, giving homeowners a lot of confidence that house prices will consistently go up. However, house prices can and do go down, and many markets across Canada have seen declines in recent years, despite the majority of markets seeing increases.

Because homes aren't a pure investment and because they are so necessarily entwined in our lives, the bad investment characteristics we discussed in Chapter 12 can also wreak havoc on retirement. The worst-case scenario would be when a homeowner is forced to sell when house prices are down. It might be because of a cash-flow issue or an inability to maintain a home, or the homeowner may need care or support that they can't arrange or afford in their home. The timing of these needs is completely unrelated to investment performance and can result in a forced sale at a low price.

In our last example, where Val and Zain were heading toward a comfortable retirement — and an even better one if they sold and chose to rent — the run-up in Toronto house prices over the past twenty years played a huge part in their financial success. With essentially all their eggs in one basket, had Toronto house prices not increased as much as they did, their retirement would look a lot less comfortable. If they were to choose not to sell and instead stay in their home, they would continue to run the risk of having the vast majority of their wealth tied up in a single investment. It's been a long time since Toronto house prices went down, but real estate is cyclical. House prices will go down at some point.

I believe a lot of retiree and senior homeowners are unlikely to sell their homes because they've spent a long time living there and they have a well-established community of friends, family, and activities. That is a choice every person is free to make. But I also think it's important to recognize the real reasons we make housing decisions so we can properly evaluate and understand why we make the decisions we are making and make sure those decisions are the right decisions for us.

Failing to appreciate the total cost of our housing can significantly affect the way we spend our retirement years. I think retirement can be a wonderful, fulfilling time in our lives, and I think Canadian retirees owe it themselves to pursue the best retirement possible.

> Failing to appreciate the total cost of our housing can significantly affect the way we spend our retirement years.

House prices across Canada have risen dramatically over the past two decades, providing homeowners with a lot of wealth. For retirees, owning a home carries significant risks, including the risk of house prices falling. More importantly, and perhaps less well understood, owning a home in retirement creates the risk that you'll spend far too much on housing, at the expense of living the retirement of your dreams. The best and easiest way to clearly understand and be aware of our housing costs is to rent. Choosing to rent might also significantly increase your income, freeing you up to explore all sorts of new interests!

# CHAPTER 20

## Seven Reasons Renting Is a Better Financial Decision

As we explored in Chapter 2, there are many, many people around us more than willing to highlight the shortcomings of renting compared to buying. But it's not a one-sided argument. There are a lot of great benefits to renting, and they deserve to be talked about. So here we go. Seven solid arguments that show renting is a better deal than buying:

### 1. NO HOUSE PRICE RISK

Houses go up and down in value depending on the time and location. When a house goes up in value, the owner wins. When it goes down, they lose.

In the investment world, the chance that an investment could go up or down is known as risk, and in the investment world, taking risk requires a reward. When you buy a house, you are taking investment risk. When you rent, you aren't. We know that a house is usually the most expensive purchase we'll ever make, so, by default, buying a house is the biggest financial risk most homeowners ever take.

There are many ways the risk of home ownership can cost you dearly, and

*If you aren't in a position to take on the very significant risk of home ownership, then you should choose the no-risk option of renting.*

depending on your circumstances — if you have irregular employment, a lack of sufficient income for a down payment, or a desire to travel and live in different places — the risk of home ownership may not be suitable for you. If you aren't in a position to take on this very significant risk, then you should choose the no-risk option of renting a place to live.

## 2. NO TRANSACTION COSTS

It depends on where you buy a house and the local and regional taxes, brokerage conventions, and regulations, but it's safe to say that any time a house is sold from one person to another, close to 10 percent of the purchase price is consumed by fees, taxes, and other expenses. Brokerage fees average about 5 percent of the purchase price and are typically paid by the seller. The land transfer tax can be between zero and 3.5 percent of the purchase price of a house and is typically paid by the buyer. Legal fees usually amount to a couple of thousand dollars, and as a percentage depends on the purchase price (roughly 1 percent for the average U.S. or Canadian house price). And there can be other expenses, like home inspections and painting.

Renting has no transaction costs, either when you move in or out. No realtor fees, no lawyers, no mortgages, no home inspection, no land transfer taxes. Nothing.

## 3. MOBILITY

Buying a house is a big commitment, and there are pros and cons to commitments. For most people, our life circumstances and housing needs change significantly over time, and there may or may not be times when it makes sense to make a significant commitment to a specific home in a specific location.

Owning a home limits your flexibility to travel, change jobs, or move to other cities or countries. It ties you to the city or town where you've bought. Houses require care and maintenance. It can take months or years to sell, and, depending on the state of the housing market, a weak housing market could make it too expensive to sell.

In contrast, renting allows the flexibility to have certainty on ending tenancy — simply giving your landlord notice provides a definitive moving date. There are no transaction costs. No dependence on the state of the housing market.

When you rent, you're mobile. When you buy, you're tied down.

## 4. NO LUMPY MAINTENANCE COSTS

When you rent, you can easily predict how much your housing is going to cost. You pay a fixed rent and you might pay some of the utilities ... and that's it. If a furnace breaks down, a roof leaks, or a foundation cracks, a renter simply calls the landlord. The landlord arranges for the repair and pays for it.

But when you buy, there's no one else to pay for the repairs but you. They can be lumpy. Costs are easily in the $10,000+ range to replace a roof or a heating and air conditioning system or to repair a foundation.

Murphy's Law says that major expenses can and will arise at precisely the worst time: the same month tuition is due, a wedding has to be paid for, an expensive medical treatment is required, or other major expenses arise. Huge, unexpected expenses are a part of life for homeowners, but renters never get hit with these.

## 5. LOWER COST

Despite the fact that there are so many advantages to renting, in every major city in Canada it costs less each month to rent than it does to buy. In many markets the cost to rent is as little as half of the cost of buying. Even when we ignore all of the additional costs of owning a home, like property taxes and maintenance, among others, the mortgage payment alone is more than 70 percent more on a monthly basis than renting a two-bedroom apartment across Canada.

> Despite the fact that there are so many advantages to renting, in every major city in Canada it costs less each month to rent than it does to buy.

It's tough to say why the gap is so wide in so many markets. Some of the gap can be attributed to the social preference for ownership over renting. Some of it can be attributed to the common perception that housing is a good investment. And some of it could be that the government consistently rewards owners through continued and new policies promoting ownership.

Whatever the reasons, renting is a more affordable option, and everyone likes to pay less. (Or at least they should!)

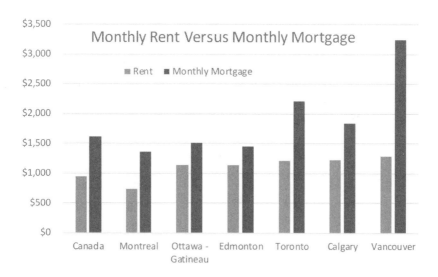

Assumptions: 5 percent down payment, five-year fixed mortgage, average MLS house price. Source: CMHC, CREA, Bank Of Canada.

## 6. NO "INVESTMENT" CREEP

A good investment is one that is made without personal bias, has no emotional aspects, and in which the purchase and sale decision is made purely based on the investment's expected return prospects. Housing doesn't meet this standard because you live in a home and take pride in it, and because your housing affects so many parts of your life.

A house may provide a good investment return. History suggests most don't. But the real problem with housing is that we confuse it with investment and end up spending too much. When most people are looking to buy a house, they start out with a budget in mind and look at some houses. Once they've seen what's available, their initial budget begins to grow. Almost without fail, the reasoning behind expanding the budget is twofold: For just a bit more money you can get a house with a lot more to offer, and housing is a place where you can justify spending more because it's an investment. That thought process is remarkably common, and it leads to all sorts of bad housing decisions. Renters never fall victim to investment creep because there is clearly no value remaining after a lease ends.

## 7. BETTER LOCATIONS

Location is a big thing in real estate. Some consider it the most important attribute of a property, and it generally plays a huge role in the price of housing. Everybody wants to live in the best location, and they're willing to pay more to live there. Partly because renting is cheaper, you can afford to live in a better location when you rent. Also, there tend to be more rental properties available in better locations — because landlords tend to know a lot about real estate, they know where to build and own rental properties.

> Because landlords know a lot about real estate, there tend to be more rental properties available in better locations.

Better locations are generally close to transit, be it highways, buses, subways, trains, or bike paths, making it easier to travel to work, recreation, or other places. Better locations have conveniences, like restaurants, grocery stores, and other stores nearby. Convenience saves time, as does good access to transit. Less time spent on commuting and shopping means more time with family and friends, relaxing or doing whatever you like to do with your free time.

◉   ◉   ◉

While these many ways in which renting is better than buying are compelling and accurate, you don't often hear them mentioned, mainly because nearly everyone involved in housing is incentivized to promote ownership. While the benefits of renting are so clear and compelling, they lack the strong advocacy that home ownership does because the primary, and often only, beneficiaries of renting are the renters themselves. This is no different than many other choices that are best for individuals or families that also don't support more consumption and spending. The things that are most advertised and promoted are all things that give others, including businesses, the opportunity to generate profits from those decisions. It is these profits that pay for the advertising and promotion dollars that fund promotion campaigns. Renting is the more logical, cheap, flexible, and low-risk way to live.

# CHAPTER 21

## How to Be a Wealthy Renter

This entire book is about how to make wise decision about housing, minimize the risks of over-consuming housing, and how you can become wealthy by never owning a home and remaining a renter your entire life. I believe that not only can you be a renter and become wealthy, but you can also become wealthy taking less risk than you would buying a home.

Statistically speaking, most Canadians will become homeowners over the course of their lives unless the future is a lot different from the past. I'm not betting on Canada becoming a nation of renters. However, whether you choose to be a renter for a short time, a long time, or your entire life, understanding the appeal of renting and how to make renting work for you can help you make better housing decisions at every point in your life.

> Understanding the differences between renting and owning can help you make better housing decisions at every point in your life.

I am a particularly big fan of renting for a reason almost everyone can appreciate: renting makes understanding financial planning much more simple and straightforward. The beauty of renting is that the rent you pay is very transparently 100-percent consumption, with no residual value — you walk away with nothing. It provides renters with a very clear understanding of how much of their income they are spending on housing, and there is no room for investment creep to confuse the situation. It also takes away the mortgage payment as an excuse to let ourselves off the hook for not being more active on financial planning. As a renter, there can be no illusion of financial security provided by our housing.

I think this is particularly important because home ownership is a significantly misunderstood thing, and it is also so heavily marketed and promoted. Real estate is a cyclical industry, and the cycles are very long. Long enough that by the time a downturn comes, most everyone has completely forgotten that it is cyclical, and they aren't prepared for the magnitude of the fall.

A misunderstood, heavily marketed, and wildly popular investment that makes up 38 percent of average Canadians' wealth (and much more than that of mortgage holders') is a recipe for disappointment. I'm not expecting a great crash in Canadian house prices, but I am expecting disappointment of one form or another. Looking at price appreciation over the past twenty years in Canada sets pretty unrealistic expectations for house prices in the future. If prices rise over the next ten years at the same 5.9 percent per year rate as the last ten years, and for the next ten years Canadian household incomes rise at the same 2.9 percent as the last ten years, average price to income ratio will reach 9.3 times. I can't see that happening, particularly with many of Canada's major cities lacking land constraints and interest rates being at all-time lows.

> Real estate is a cyclical industry, and the cycles are very long. Long enough that by the time a downturn comes, most everyone has completely forgotten that it is cyclical, and they aren't prepared for the magnitude of the fall.

Yet, while renting simplifies the task of understanding housing, there is also no wealth built through renting itself. Renters need to put in place a savings program that can replicate the forced savings program that home ownership includes.

It's pretty much that simple: Put a savings program in place that will build wealth over time and let it work for you. I firmly believe the combination of renting and a forced savings program should provide a strong financial outlook, and one that is significantly stronger than one that relies on home ownership.

I don't care if you rent or if you own. I don't care if you live in the city, in the country, or somewhere in between. And I don't care if you choose high-rise living, single-family, or any other form of housing. What I do care about is that you know as much as possible about the housing decisions you face, before you make them, so you can make the best, most informed housing decisions possible.

Regardless of whether you buy or rent, there are some key concepts I hope have come through clearly as you've read this book and that I think are critical to understanding housing choices.

1.  The decision to become a homeowner, or the decision to not become a homeowner, is the biggest financial decision you are likely to make in your entire life.

2.  The cards are stacked against you. Virtually every source of advice on housing is biased: from the government, which prefers you own, to agents, who want you to transact quickly, to family, who want you to have the safety net of forced savings, to even the economists who are calling for a crash in prices. Housing is a complicated thing, and there are no good sources of advice. Renting is the best way to neutralize all of this bad advice.

3.  If you decide to be a renter, find a forced savings program that works for you. Preferably more than one. Having forced savings will ensure you build wealth over time and have a secure financial future.

4.  If you decide to be a homeowner, take your time, figure out what you want from housing, and wait for the right opportunity. Buying the wrong house is very expensive.

5.  If you're going to buy a home, figure out how much the land you are buying represents as a percentage of the purchase price so you can get a sense of long-term return potential. If the financial performance of your housing is a top priority, try to maximize the value of the land in your purchase.

6.  Be aware of and consciously try to avoid investment creep. Renting is the best way to avoid investment creep. For homebuyers, it's easy to let it creep in and leave you house poor. Whether you rent or buy, have a budget and a list of features that you want, and resist the urge to spend more to get more. Housing is a consumption item!

7. Try to minimize the number of times you buy and sell houses. Transaction costs are huge, particularly when you consider the impact relative to your equity in a home with a mortgage. Spending the time to make the right choices should help you achieve this goal. Renting also massively reduces this cost.

8. Know how much rent you are paying — whether it's to yourself because you own your home outright, to the bank because you have a mortgage, or to a landlord because you are renting. This is an important piece of financial information too many people don't have.

9. Try to get as much of your total asset base into assets that both go up in value and provide income (like dividend-paying stocks), and as little of it as possible into the depreciating, negative-cash-flow category. The more you can do that, the more wealth you'll build over time.

I hope reading this book has helped you understand more about how housing works, and that you are better prepared to make the right decisions when it comes to your housing. I have one final piece of advice for you: The best defence against biased advice is knowledge. Learn as much as you can about your housing options, from as many different sources as you can, to make sure your housing decisions are the best decisions you can make and to ensure housing, in whatever form you choose, makes you happy, healthy, and wealthy.

# INDEX

# DUNDURN

VISIT US AT

*Dundurn.com*
*@dundurnpress*
*Facebook.com/dundurnpress*
*Pinterest.com/dundurnpress*